GOD CHOSE ME

GOD CHOSE ME

UNTOUCHABLE CONFIDENCE
FOR THE UNSTOPPABLE CHRISTIAN

CHARLES H. METCALF III

Foreword by
New York Times *bestselling author Michael Todd*

WaterBrook

WaterBrook

An imprint of the Penguin Random House Christian Publishing Group,
a division of Penguin Random House LLC

1745 Broadway, New York, NY 10019

waterbrookmultnomah.com
penguinrandomhouse.com

Library of Congress Cataloging-in-Publication Data
Names: Metcalf, Charles Henry, III, author. | Todd, Michael (Pastor), writer of foreword.
Title: God chose me: untouchable confidence for the unstoppable christian/
Charles Henry Metcalf, III;
foreword by Michael Todd.
Description: First edition. | [Colorado Springs] : WaterBrook, [2025] |
Includes bibliographical references.
Identifiers: LCCN 2024060673 | ISBN 9780593603185 (hardcover) | ISBN 9780593603192 (ebook)
Subjects: LCSH: Self-confidence—Religious aspects—Christianity. |
Self-acceptance—Religious aspects—Christianity.
Classification: LCC BV4598.23 .M49 2025 | DDC 248.4—dc23/eng/20250216
LC record available at https://lccn.loc.gov/2024060673

Printed in the United States of America on acid-free paper

2 4 6 8 9 7 5 3 1

First Edition

The authorized representative in the EU for product safety and compliance is
Penguin Random House Ireland, Morrison Chambers, 32 Nassau Street, Dublin D02 YH68,
Ireland. https://eu-contact.penguin.ie

BOOK TEAM: Editor: Drew Dixon • Production editor: Helen Macdonald •
Managing editor: Julia Wallace • Production manager: Mark Maguire •
Copy editor: Lisa Grimenstein • Proofreaders: Bailey Utecht, Drew Goter

For details on special quantity discounts for bulk purchases, contact
specialmarketscms@penguinrandomhouse.com.

Author's Note

I wrote this book with extreme care and vulnerability. Its origin is a very painful and dark place for me, and that place serves as the opening for this book. For anyone struggling with anxiety, depression, or suicidal thoughts, I want you to know I've been there. Throughout these pages, I will share my journey. Please proceed with caution as I know some parts may be triggering. I pray that as I share some of these real struggles, you will find healing and hope to face the most painful parts of your life with the power and peace I found in the message "God chose me."

Foreword

There are certain people you can tell are special from the moment you meet them. You know they will change the world. When you hear them speak, you can tell they have something profound to say. When they talk about their future, you imagine great things for them. Or, in the case of Charles Henry Metcalf, III, you meet that one person who can take any assortment of clothes and make a fashion statement.

The beautiful thing about Charles is that he fulfills every category I just mentioned. He is a great man.

Let me tell you about how I met Charles.

It was 2017 and I had just finished preaching a sermon at the local church I lead, Transformation Church. I was tired but really excited about all the people who had come and experienced our little growing church. Part of my pastoral duties is to care for and love my fellow brothers and sisters in Christ. Part of my big brother duties is to care for and love my blood brothers.

After our church service was over that night, my youngest brother, Graceson, asked me to drive him to another church service. My initial thought was, *Another church service?* I mean, what church could he be going to after such a dynamic, magnificent spiritual gathering of the saints, where lives were forever transformed, being led to perfection by his older brother? But I tried to act unbothered and agreed to take him.

During the drive, I asked him about the church, called Eden. He told me about this amazing new church plant that was filled with creatives helping to change lives. He went on and on about how much he loved this new church and the cool, trendy pastors (Charles and Abby Metcalf) who preached so well—and *everybody* was going there.

I thought, I'm *not there.*

I knew I should be grateful that my brother wanted to go to church multiple times a day instead of not at all. But this experience had me wondering, *Who is this Charles Metcalf?* I tracked him down through social media and realized my little brother was right: Charles was cool. He was smart. And, more than anything else, he seemed to have a genuine understanding of God's Word and a love for God's people.

That intrigued me enough to invite Charles to breakfast. Before I met with him, I asked God to tell me what our relationship was supposed to look like. I felt God tell me to help Charles and give him whatever he needed. When we met, we had the most captivating conversation. We had so much in common—music, sports, fashion, God's Word, and more. Almost instantly, it felt like something special was happening.

I had this weird feeling that we were supposed to be connected.

I felt that connection so deeply that by the end of the meeting, I asked Charles if he would ever consider partnering to do ministry together. I used this elaborate analogy about the Golden State Warriors when Stephen Curry, Kevin Durant, Draymond Green, and Klay Thompson played together, asking Charles if he wanted to do ministry as a team instead of separately. In the kindest, most amazing matter-of-fact way, Charles declined. And so, I decided to cheer him on from the sidelines.

Fast-forward several months as he and his wife prepared to open their church and my little brother was still asking me to drop him off at Eden each week. I felt God call me to attend a training for pastors in Dallas, Texas, and that I was supposed to pay for Charles to come as a future leader of Eden. I asked if he'd join me and he agreed, and we spent the next four days sharing meals, gaining understanding, and building camaraderie.

During our time together, I witnessed a life-altering moment for Charles. In an act of what I call crazy faith, Charles and his wife, Abby, decided to close the flourishing and life-giving church they were starting, in order to, in his own words, "serve and protect." This was a moment that I will refer to only as "Is he really crying on my shoulder in Neiman Marcus?" Maybe one day we'll share the entire story of how God brought two regular guys together to represent Him to the world.

As I watched Charles navigate, sacrifice, and submit to the process that God was inviting him into, I realized I had never seen such resolute faith at such a young age. He did not waver in what God had asked of him. He obeyed, and it was almost as if God was marking him for a special assignment not just for him but for his entire generation and other generations as well. It was as if God had *chosen* him. Throughout history, God has marked people. Throughout Scripture, God marked people. Today, God marks people. In fact, I believe God marks everybody. The question is not whether God marked you, but rather, Will you answer the call?

I believe that through Charles's wisdom, creativity, illustrations, and lifestyle, you will learn principles that are practical as well as profound. These principles will help you step into all the possibilities that align with your God-given purpose and recognize the greatness that God has placed in you to touch the world.

I have watched Charles preach and write this message, which is a feat all by itself. But I have also watched him live this message. If you apply just half of the godly gold that is shared on the forthcoming pages, you will inevitably be transformed.

Charles, I am proud of you for you. I am for you. I will stand with you. I love you—and not because of anything that you'd done, written, said, or shown me. But simply because I love you.

Oh, and by the way, God chose you.

—Michael Todd

Contents

GOD CHOSE ME

Prologue

THE BOOK STARTS NOW

I feel the faint buzzing of flying at thirty thousand feet. Ambient music hums through my corded headphones, and the inside of my eyelids start to sparkle with a rainbow of fireworks after being closed for too long. My fingers are on the laptop keyboard, and my wife sits next to me, the smell of her perfume drifting into my nostrils, the most comforting scent on the planet. My heart thuds as recycled air brushes my shoulder. Deep breath in . . . and out. *You can do this. Just calm down and write.*

I have written and rewritten this first paragraph too many times to count. Word documents, journals, scribbles, napkins, iPhone notes, even on the outside of a Starbucks cup—all filled with attempts at the opening of this book as I search for a way to do this idea justice. I sense it so clearly. I know in my heart how reading this book should *feel*, but it's all stuck in my head. I can sense the emotion deep within my bones. There's only one problem: *You can't feel what I feel. You can't see what I see.* And so I find myself struggling to convey my message with words that will make sense. Time and again I type, write, delete, scribble, rewrite, and adjust. Over and over.

Why?

I care. I care at a depth that is difficult to relate. I wish I could say I couldn't care less whether you like this book, but that wouldn't be true. I care deeply.

I am keenly aware that I have only a short period of time to grab your attention. That pressure is heightened because the fire with which this message burns in my bones cannot be contained. I feel a holy conviction to share the message of this book—a message that I believe has the potential to change your life. At the same time, I feel an unreasonable pressure to prove myself—to you, to the publisher, to your friends and my friends, to the people who didn't believe in me . . . to the world. I feel I must prove that this message is worth all the hard work.

Out of all the pressure, there is one person's gaze that weighs heaviest. I hear his comments, expectations, judgments, critiques, criticisms. I feel his scrutiny as it pierces my very soul, as if to say, "Come on, let's see it." I restart a sentence, and he rolls his eyes. He scoffs every time I misspell a word. He's been with me as long as I can remember. He's quick to point out my flaws, quirks, and brokenness. Even at my best, there's always *something* I could've done different or better. It is this person, most of all, whom I must prove wrong. I must show him I am not who he has said I am. Who he has seen.

This person . . . is me.

It's not the pressure from others that has me writing and rewriting. It's my own thoughts, my own insecurities, fears, deficiencies, my own ideas of what my first book should sound like.

But more than that, I want this book to matter. To make an impact. To make a difference and to be of value. I didn't spend all this time and energy just to scribble nonsense. I did it because I believe this book has the potential to change your life. But do I have what it takes to help you see that?

Sometimes I am filled with an overwhelming sense of confidence to trust that the God of the universe is inspiring and empowering me to write these words. Other times I feel a paralyzing uncertainty.

And that's the point.

That internal battle, that perpetual conflict, that all-out *war*— that is why I am writing this book.

We have all felt it at different times. That internal pressure that randomly surfaces, even in your greatest moments. The questions that pop up just as you're drifting into peaceful sleep. Questions of the soul and pressures of existence—these are the seeds of this book.

Do I have what it takes?

Will I fail again?

How can I harness the potential that lies dormant within?

What is the source of my confidence and reassurance?

Will I make it?

Will my family be okay?

Am I enough?

What will happen to my children?

Will I always be alone?

Do I have good ideas?

Will people read my book?

Can I do this?

How do I find my way in this world of opinions, deception, pressure, and anxiety? In a world where bad news seems to be the only news, fear is common, and hope is a distant memory? How do I muster up the courage and confidence to be who I was created to be?

The words and chapters that follow are born from the same place that my opening paragraph was written: a place of humility, openness, and transparency. But let me be clear—this is not because humble, open, and transparent is who I've always been. Rather, it is the version of myself I have learned to be. This book is about learning to believe the deepest truth about ourselves, the truth that is the only real and lasting answer to the fears, insecurities, and pressures we face every day.

My hope is that within these pages, you'll discover the supernatural source that has radically changed my life. I pray that you will feel the transformational power of a God who strengthens the weak and gives hope to the weary. That ultimately you would unlock an untouchable confidence to live as an unstoppable Christian.

It is my deep conviction that the Spirit of God can empower any believer to live a life full of confidence and contentment. A life where they are not shaken by circumstance or opinion but live with a fire that cannot be extinguished.

I believe that as you step into this supernatural confidence, you will become an unstoppable force in the world.

On this journey, you'll experience trials, joy, fear, laughter, and much more. But I am confident you have *everything* you need within you to reach this reality.

My goal is not to conjure up some self-helped, self-willed self-acceptance that comes from *you,* as amazing as that is and as strong as your self-will might be. History has proven that humans are far too fickle to be trusted. My hope is to give you a source of confidence that transcends race and religion, gender and class, political party, 401(k) plans, and education. I want to impart to you something extraordinarily simple yet with extravagant implications: a source of true confidence that is not dependent on circumstance, praise, or approval and a lasting contentment that goes beyond momentary happiness to a deep inner joy and hope.

Just imagine for a moment: a life free of the worry about what other people think about you. A day where you wake up extremely confident in who you are and what you were placed on this planet to do. Where the opinions of others do not keep you bound to the safety of what you know. Where you are not hindered by a second-guessing gait. Where you wake up full of vision, hope, and a sense of eternal destiny. Where the fear of failing does not paralyze you, but rather you run free and full of the God-given power within you. What would that life be like? How would you talk and walk? What would that version of you do? It is this version that lies on the other side of the decision to believe "God Chose Me."

As we journey together, I want to ask you a question that will take a lot of courage to answer. (Only a few pages in and I am already requiring something from you! But the people who love me most always ask something of me. And *I love you*.)

But first, close your eyes.

Take a deep breath: Four seconds in . . . hold for four . . . release for four. (Go ahead, I'll wait.)

Here's my request: Be present and be patient.

I have been a speaker, teacher, and preacher of the message of Jesus for a little more than a decade now. My journey has had some hilariously embarrassing moments and a few special highlights. During my time as a communicator, I have always been a learner. I've read more books, listened to more podcasts, and borrowed more techniques than I can count. One of the most helpful pieces of advice I've heard was from a speaker. Judah Smith said, "The greatest thing you can do before you speak to an audience of any size is to fall in love with the moment and fall in love with the people. You speak differently in a moment you love and to a people you love."

More than any other words of advice, that piece of wisdom has shaped me. Falling in love with right now allows me to forget my fears, worries, and ideas about what *should* happen. It takes the pressure off.

That's really what I want to say to you.

Take the pressure off.

Whatever you are hoping to get or change about yourself from reading this book is not nearly as important as being present in and to this moment. If you're anything like me, you have spent a significant portion of your life stuck in negative thought patterns that have sabotaged your self-worth and confidence. As you begin to rewire your thoughts, it will take time to become the version of yourself that does not default to these broken systems. However, I am confident that with time and commitment and the help of a gracious God you will be surprised at how this journey transforms not only you but the way you see the world.

So, let us begin what I hope will be one of the most transformative and powerful journeys of your life—the journey to an untouchable confidence for an unstoppable Christian.

Chapter 1

You Are Loved at Your Lowest

This is the end. It's over. Your time has come. The plane is going down and no one else is to blame. There is nothing left to do. You are going down, this is it. This is the end of your story.
—Personal journal, April 2020

M y body physically remembers the hopelessness I felt when I wrote those words. I was curled underneath my desk at work, writing what I believed would be the final journal entry and letter to those I left behind. I felt alone, hopeless and helpless. My soul felt as dark as the ocean floor, and the pressure was crushing me. I felt like I couldn't breathe. No matter how much I wanted things to be different, this was it. This was my reality. At the age of twenty-six, I was going to take my own life.

I found myself stuck in the tension of who I was, who I could be, and who I wanted to be. For as long as I can remember, there has been a war going on inside of me. A quiet yet tumultuous war between two stories. In one story I was happy, full of life. I made the best choices for my life, lived joyfully, and stayed committed to my values. In the other story, I cast off all responsibility. I gave up trying to achieve and essentially said forget it. I did what I wanted, when I wanted. Why? Because I didn't want the pressure of who I "could be." I don't know the genesis of this war; however, this internal battle had ravaged my soul so much that the idea of giving up felt far more realistic than continuing to fight. I believed that something was broken or missing in me and that there was no chance I would ever find the missing pieces that everyone else seemed to have.

I grew up going to church, so I know the Bible. The Scriptures contain a book of songs, titled Psalms, primarily written by a man named David. The 150 songs found in this book convey the whole gamut of human emotion—from the beauty and joy of victory to even anguish and deep frustration with God. I titled what I thought was my last journal entry "Psalm 151." This was my last hope and appeal to God. The pain, turmoil, and emptiness had become so overwhelming, and I saw no other option but to end my life. The letter I wrote reflects how far I felt from God, from hope, from living. I saw no light at the end of my tunnel. Let me give you a little backstory to help you understand how I got here.

2020: "THE YEAR THAT CHANGED THE WORLD"

It was 2020 and, like everyone else, I was having a typical year.

Until I wasn't.

The fabric of the earth, society, media, health, truth—everything—seemed to split wide-open with no hope or help in sight in March of 2020. We plunged into a global pandemic that shut down our world in an unparalleled manner. Physical sickness turned political as people grasped for power over the virus. The debate of mask-or-no-mask became the divider of households. Racial tensions spun out of control. George Floyd cried out to his mother. There were riots in the streets in response to the many instances where police had shot black men and women over the

years. It seemed as if every evil, twisted, dark plan had been un-
leashed simultaneously and we were all caught in this tornado,
not knowing which way was up or down. No matter your "side,"
there was a general sense of chaos that seemed to cut through the
safety and sense of security we all desperately cling to.

Like for many others during this time, my place of work moved
to my home. The only problem? I didn't have a home. Or rather, I
had a roof over my head; it just wasn't mine. I was living in the
bonus room of my in-laws' house with my fifteen-month-old son
and eight-months-pregnant wife. My in-laws' offer to let us stay
with them at this time was one of the kindest acts of generosity
toward our growing family. (Thank you, Mom and BC!)

I was navigating the waters of being stuck in one place, a complete lack of socialization, and worries about whether my family
would be safe. During this time, while I was practicing social dis-
tancing to protect myself and my family, I failed to realize I was
also growing distant from something else: God. I am not sure
when or how it happened, but His voice drifted into the background and all the other worries of life took over. I could no longer see His hand or feel His love. I grew cold, empty, and hopeless,
becoming a shell of the joy and laughter I once carried. My once
boisterous spirit slowly began to fade into a deep depression. It
was as though I had a slow leak in my tire. I found myself stranded
in a place I did not recognize, with no clear way out.

The combination of all these feelings manifested as unpredict-
able panic attacks. I didn't realize it at the time, but my soul was
screaming for help like a hostage tied up in the darkest room. No
one could hear, no one could see, and I was too unaware to ask for
the help I needed. What started as a fuzzy feeling in my mind grew
to an unceasing hurricane of fear and whirling thoughts. Thinking that maybe I just needed more sleep, I took sleep medicine—

but that was useless. My body was tired, but my mind kept on racing. This storm turned into a heaviness in my chest, a weight on my shoulders, a heat behind my ears, and a tingle in my hands. Every six hours or so, I would suddenly be propelled onto what felt like my last roller-coaster ride. I would shake, struggle to breathe, fall to my knees, and cry out for my wife, who would come running to hold me until I stopped trembling. It was my first time experiencing the humiliation and debilitation of a panic attack.

I vividly remember one night in particular.

FOUR A.M. FRIENDS

I had been fighting demons all day, on the verge of a panic attack throughout meetings and calls, and I finally made it home to my safe place. I had dinner with my family and a laugh with my son. Then I walked into our bedroom closet, and it hit—the spinning at the front of my mind, the pounding of my heart, the weight on my neck. My legs gave out and I fell to the floor. Yelling for help as though I were getting mugged, I curled into a ball and waited for my wife, Abby. She came and hugged me, brought me a cold rag, and rubbed my neck, but it wouldn't stop. My mind kept spinning, I couldn't breathe, and my vision was blurry. It was terrifying. She helped me stumble to our bed, where I curled into the fetal position, shaking and crying uncontrollably. In an effort to end the terror, I closed my eyes and drifted into a panicked sleep.

I awoke to voices whispering in the background. It was 2 A.M. I felt a strong hand on the back of my neck. "Charles, we're all here." I immediately felt relief—and shame. It was my friends. My wife had called them in the middle of the night. They had gotten out of bed, loaded up their children, and were now in my bedroom. Aaron was standing at the foot of the bed. Mike was to my left, sitting on my nightstand. Natalie was behind him. Abby was sitting by me, and on my left was Brie.

I have the strongest and most incredible friends ever. They are each influential and powerful in their own way. Each has their own set of divinely contracted superpowers. I love them, and they love me. But I also *admire* them. And truthfully, I wanted them to admire me too. I wanted them to think I was impressive, to feel that I could handle whatever life threw at me. And yet here I was, falling apart in my own house. I felt insignificant, embarrassed, and small.

This can't be happening, I thought to myself. *What if I lose my job, my title, my leadership?* "See? I told you . . . you aren't enough. You can't handle it" said my internal critic. *What if people start to second-guess whether I'm cut out for this role and ministry altogether? What is wrong with me?*

Just as I uttered those silent words in my head, Brie said aloud, "Charles, there is *nothing* wrong with you."

I broke. Salty tears began to stream down my face as my body slowly stopped its tremor. It wasn't Brie who was talking to me. I mean, it was—but I knew it also wasn't. There is only one man who has a track record of knowing our thoughts. There is only one person kind enough to hear our cries and answer through a friend. Jesus spoke to me. He comforted my broken heart and lifted my weary head. He was the deep breath I couldn't take and the strength I needed to see another day. In that one moment He looked past my hurt and saw my pain. He validated and valued who I was, just as I was. For the next two hours, my friends comforted and encouraged me. They spoke life-giving words over me and left notes all over my house, encouraging me toward light and hope.

There is much more to this story. More panic attacks. Many

more fears. A long journey of counseling, accountability, rest, and finding out who I really was. But what I want to highlight is this: I was loved at my lowest. When I felt the least worthy, the least capable, the least qualified, and least likely to be chosen, it was at that very moment I realized I am still loved. At my lowest. At my worst. When the pain hits like a ton of bricks. When my talent is of no use. When money has no value and when it seems I have nothing to offer but myself.

That's the moment I found out I am loved. That's when I knew God Chose Me.

The words "there is nothing wrong with you" planted a seed of hope. A seed I desperately needed, one that would grow into the garden of words that you read on this page! Maybe there could be a different ending to my story. Maybe this wasn't all life held for me. Maybe God did have something more for me than living in fear of panic attacks. Maybe I would make it through this season, and maybe life was worth living.

You Are Loved at Your Lowest

At your lowest, you are loved.

I don't know your story. I don't know the details of your journey. I know neither the demons you fight nor the struggles you face. I don't know the names of those who have left you or the trauma that has plagued you. You very well may have experienced such darkness and hopelessness that even my suggestion that something different is possible feels insulting. Or perhaps your life seems fine—great job, great friends, great future—but if you were honest, you still struggle to love yourself for who you really are. Regardless of who or how old you are, I know the human experience unites us all. We have each at one point felt the fear and darkness that cannot be answered with a quick fix. A pain that takes us to the pit we cannot see past. It is this pit and this pain where I found hope. The very hope I want to give you.

If God can find me curled up in my bed with my life spinning out of control and speak to me through my friend, He can use me to speak life into you.

You Are Worth It

You are worthy of being chosen not because you are perfect but because you are a person. And you're not just any person—you are His. God is madly in love with you, and He has a plan for your life. No matter how dark it may seem, no matter how far gone you may feel, there is no place God will not go to find those He loves. He specializes in finding, choosing, and restoring those who are lost. And you are no different.

There's a story in the Bible about a man named Hosea. It illustrates how God continues to chase and choose those who are broken and undeserving. Hosea, a leader and a prophet, was commanded by God to marry Gomer, a prostitute (see Hosea 1:1–3). Yes, you read that right. God told Hosea to marry a prostitute. (Who says the Bible is boring? People who have never read it.) Despite Hosea's best effort to love her and create a safe home for her, Gomer repeatedly left Hosea to return to the illicit life she knew. Yet, somehow, in all this turmoil and pain, Hosea never lost his love for her. At one point, Gomer fell into such degradation that she is sold as a sex slave. Hosea, in his deep love and adoration, searched the city to find her. (I wonder how far he had to go. What rooms did he have to search? What did he see and who did he have to ask, "Have you seen my wife?") He finally found her, bought her back, and restored her as his beloved wife.

Friend, this is a picture of our God. There is no place too dark, no area too dirty, where God will not go to find you.

You Are Loved Just as You Are

Wherever you are, you are loved at that place. God's love knows no bounds.

With the bottle in your hand—you are loved.

With the needle in your arm—you are loved.

Lying in their bed—you are loved.

With hate in your heart—you are loved.

After the divorce—you are loved.

After they left—you are loved.

After the public failure—you are loved.

At the very bottom of the bottom—you are loved.

Perhaps the most famous scripture of all time, John 3:16, says that "God so loved the world that he gave his one and only Son" (NIV). You need to know you are "so loved." Not for anything you have done or can do but simply for who you are. This world often tells us that our value comes from what we have done—the money we have earned or the success we have achieved. But none of those things are strong enough to anchor our soul. People, power, positions, and paper are weak counterfeits that let us down every time. They serve as artificial anchors that often break when we need them most. Above all, we need to know that we are loved and chosen without any of these things.

Do not give in to the lie that there is nothing to live for. There is beauty, there is light—there *is* a life where you know you are loved and are able to love yourself. No matter where you may be, there is a better day ahead. A day when confidence is your primary operating system. A day when you're willing to trust people and lean into relationships. A day when the hurt of the past does not keep you from the possibility of the future. A day when you speak your mind and don't back down. And that day is closer than you think.

Before you try to dig yourself out of this hole, before you try to power yourself away from this brokenness, before you move, know this:

If you never leave this place, you will still be loved.

You may think this sounds crazy. Perhaps it doesn't make sense. But it's true. You are loved—where you are, who you are, how you are. If you never beat the addiction, if you never do "the right thing," if you stay in this exact spot, you will still be loved. This love is unexplainable. It defies reason. That is because it is not an earthly love but one that finds its source in *the* source of all light and love. It is not yours to earn. It can only be accepted.

This is the gospel message: The gift of grace was purchased by the death of God's only Son, Jesus Christ. You are loved unconditionally and have been given an opportunity at a fresh start in life. A life where you do not carry the shame and burden of your mistakes. A life where, at the moment of surrender, you can experience a joy and forgiveness that frees you to move forward. As you accept this love, you will begin to see who you really are. You will discover the most valuable and special parts of how God made you. Only when you accept and see that you are loved can you stand up and stand out in this world.

I Believe, but You Don't Have To

It's important that I pause here and address those of you who still have questions about God, the church, Christians, or all of the above. I wrestled with a deep tension while writing this book. When I first began, I wanted to ensure this book would not exclude anyone who wanted to read it. I wanted the title, subtitle, and even the language throughout to be as inclusive as possible. As I worded and reworded the subtitle, I came to a decision that changed the course of my life and this book.

We Died for This Word

I was sitting in a coffee shop, on the phone with a dear friend. As I worked through my ideology and theology for the subtitle of this book, I shared how I had received feedback that using the word *Christian* might keep some people from reading it. I know many people have legitimate pain and trauma associated with that word. As I contemplated whether to include it, I was struck with a soul-jarring reality that came in the form of five words: *We died for this word.*

And as I sat there in my corner booth, I began to cry. I thought of the early church. I imagined the family whose door was being beaten down by Roman soldiers. I pictured the father sweeping his children and wife behind him as he opened the door to the soldier's shout: "Are you a Christian? Do you follow this Jesus from Nazareth and the message of His radical followers?"

The man's quiet but bold reply: "Yes, yes I do. I believe He rose from the grave and that He is the way. I follow Him. Yes, I am a Christian."

And then I imagined the Roman sword piercing through his chest. His lifeless body falling to the ground as his wife and children scream at what they'd just witnessed. His body being dragged into the street as an example to the community.

The message? Professing this word could cost you your life.

To be clear, untold number of martyrs in the early church and all of church history did not die for a word. They died for their belief in the Man behind the word. They died for rejecting human authority and embracing Jesus as their king. This word being uttered by members of the early church was no small thing. They knew what it meant. Yet they did not back down from the likely consequence of confessing it.

I realize that I am not at great risk for becoming a martyr for the gospel. As a follower of Jesus in America, I have never experienced persecution at the level I just described—persecution that many across the globe still face today. However, I do share their conviction that I will not shy away from this word. I understand it may be offensive, harsh, or hurtful to some. But I am a Christian. I am a follower of Jesus Christ, and I believe He is who He says He is.

I don't know where you are in your relationship with God, faith, or religion. Considering how many people are frustrated or disappointed with Christianity and the church, you might have a complicated and conflicted past when it comes to God. However, I want to make two things clear.

First, as stated earlier, I believe in Jesus. I believe He is the Son of God and *the* way to eternal life. I believe that His Word is true, that it is the ultimate authority on life, and that it was written with love and clarity to promote human flourishing. This doesn't mean I don't have questions or that following Jesus has solved all my problems. In fact, I have found that following Him has a clear and sometimes frustrating cost. But I cannot deny what He has done in my life. And for that, I trust Him.

Second, even if you do not believe in Christ, you can benefit from reading this book. This book is written from the conviction that truth is truth, whether it is observed or acknowledged. Whether or not you believe in God, you can still have something to gain from the idea that He chose you. That He cares for you. That out of all the people on the planet, He sees *you*. I have never met anyone who did not benefit from being seen and loved. (Especially when He happens to be the creator of the universe.) If you question His existence or the validity of the Bible, I invite you to table your skepticism for a moment. Give yourself the space to ponder the implications and impact that this truth—that God sees you and chooses you—could have on your life. If you get to the end of this book and determine that this message is not useful to your flourishing, we can happily part ways and I will still love you and believe the best for you. Deal?

I have learned that it is extremely difficult to believe that you are chosen if you do not first grasp that you are loved. Loved because of who you are and not what you do. It is from this place of vulnerability that God can begin His most beautiful work in your soul. As my friend Tobe would say, "Try Jesus." Jesus is a great friend and a better savior. If you are at the end of yourself, you just might find the beginning of Him. He is kind, He is gracious, and He can save you and your situation. It's what He does. He picks the worst and does His best.

Still don't believe me? Let me introduce you to some friends.

Chapter 2

THIS IS WHAT GOD DOES

Even before I was born, God chose me and called me by his marvelous grace.
— Paul, Galatians 1:15

If you have difficulty believing God could choose you, I invite you to consider the following list.

A drunk

A liar

An old man with no future

A stuttering criminal

A prostitute

A murderer navigating the aftermath of an affair

A ragtag group of twelve rejects

A teenage girl

A religious hit man

As random as this list may seem, it includes some of my favorite individuals of all time. Heroes, you could say. They all have diverse backgrounds, stories, and lives. However, one essential detail unites them: They were all chosen by God.

THE WORST START-UP EVER

Let's say you are starting a company. It's a small operation, but the mission is global and has a high upside. You spend years establishing your game plan, discussing it with your two other investors. After what seems like hundreds of years of preparation, you finally launch. You have a rough start, but after a few years, it gets rolling. Right before you are about to go to market, you realize this vision is bigger than you expected, and you need to recruit some teammates. Again, this is a big deal. You have put your everything into this and have waited for the perfect timing, and this is your one shot to make it happen. As you begin the interview process, you have many great candidates. After a day full of interviews, you gather as an investment team, and your biggest investor and final decision-maker lays out the list of top choices to get the mission done. He proceeds to rattle off the list of broken individuals I shared earlier as his top choices and the core team with whom you will launch this business.

Overwhelmed and concerned for the future of the company, you look into the eyes of your biggest investor. You have one question for the boss: "Why are you taking such a massive risk on these people who are clearly unqualified?"

He heaves a deep sigh, leans forward in his chair, and says, "I am not taking a risk on them. I am making a bet on myself."

THIS IS WHAT GOD DOES

My friend, this is God. The list I referred to earlier is not some made-up assortment of individuals. Instead, these are a few of the most important and influential leaders of the movement of faith and message of Jesus. His "dream team," if you will. As crazy as that sounds, it is the truth. This is what God does and who He is. He chooses the unqualified to do the miraculous. It is the way He started His plan, it's the way He sustained it, and it will be the way He continues to bring the life-giving message of hope to the world. God specializes in choosing messed-up, jacked-up, twisted, unqualified people.

THE BEST OF THE WORST

Let's meet some of these folks. The old man with no future is better known as Abraham. The father of the faith. When God found him, he was living in a pagan land with his family. He had no children and no future. It was at this moment God called him out from his tent and told him to look up into the sky. As many stars as he could see, so would be his descendants (see Genesis 15). He went on to be the father of a nation and part of the lineage that would bring about the Savior, Jesus.

The drunk is Noah. We know him as the one who built a boat that saved the last pure-hearted individuals on the planet and two of every animal to launch a fresh start after the world was flooded. But Genesis 9 tells about this lesser-known incident of Noah's drunkenness.

The liar's name was Jacob before it was changed to Israel ("the one who struggles") after a wrestling match with God. He started his career by conspiring with his mother to lie to his dad and cheat his older brother out of their father's blessing (see Genesis 27). A horrible act—and yet, God still chose him and used him to bring about the twelve tribes of Israel, God's chosen people.

The stuttering criminal, otherwise known as Moses, led two million people out of slavery after four hundred years.

The prostitute, Rahab, risked her own life to protect two of God's chosen leaders and is intentionally listed in the genealogy of Jesus, reminding us how our savior came into this broken world.

The adulterer who killed the husband of the woman he cheated with? David. One of the best songwriters, poets, kings, and leaders in human history. He was even called "a man after [God's] own heart" (Acts 13:22).

The teenage girl? Mary, who birthed Jesus, our savior, into this world.

And finally, the religious hit man, aka Christian-killer? That's Paul, who wrote much of the New Testament, planted churches across the world, and went down as one of the most influential people to shape our faith.

Do you get it? Do you see it? This is what He does. This is who He is. He intentionally chooses the least, the smallest, the unqualified, the overlooked, and the underestimated.

The question now is, Why? Does He have some ego complex? Poor judgment? I mean, really, what's the deal?

If you want the answer to this question, look no further than a letter written by our once-murderous friend Paul.

God Chooses Nobodies

Do you feel foolish, weak, or lowly? Friend, I've got good news. You are the ideal candidate to be chosen and used by God to turn the world upside down.

> God chose the foolish things of the world to shame the wise; God chose the weak things of the world to shame the strong. God chose the lowly things of this world and the despised things—and the things that are not—to nullify the things that are, so that no one may boast before him. (1 Corinthians 1:27–29, NIV)

If you relate to any portion of this scripture, you are perfectly positioned to see the power of God move in your life. He can take your regular, mundane, and even painful life and bring peace, power, and purpose to it. He can take the parts of you that seem too broken and turn them into your greatest strengths. God does not need the best and the brightest to accomplish His work on earth.

One of the biggest myths in the world says that only great people can be great and only select individuals can be used by God. This could not be further from the truth. God loves choosing those who seem underestimated and unnoticed. I love Eugene Peterson's *The Message* translation of 1 Corinthians 1:27–29:

> I don't see many of "the brightest and the best" among you, not many influential, not many from high-society families. Isn't it obvious that God deliberately chose men and women that the culture overlooks and exploits and abuses, chose these "nobodies" to expose the hollow pretensions of the "somebodies"?

God chooses nobodies. This is the gospel. This is the good news. God is in the business of choosing nobodies to show those who think they are "somebody" what really matters. That's just

God. Time and again, this is what He does. Because this is who He is.

So what does this mean for you and me? The things we think disqualify us from being chosen are the very things God is planning to use in our lives. What if the very thing you think disqualifies you from purpose is the platform God wants to use to reveal His glory through you? What if the pain you have worked so hard to hide is the thing God wants to use to show His goodness to your friends? What if your worst moment is God's best moment? What if your weakest weakness is nothing compared to God's strength? What if God really can use anybody to do anything? And better yet, what if that somebody isn't just anybody? What if it's *you*?

When you begin to recognize and embrace this pattern of God, it will transform the perspectives in your mind and heart. This small but significant revelation gives you permission to step into any season or situation with true confidence. You no longer have a list of things you are trying to hide from God, things you have decided He can't use. Instead, you see things differently. Rather than hiding your weaknesses and failures, you actually take them out and put them on display.

MY DIRT IS ON DISPLAY

Imagine you are having a bunch of people over for dinner and instead of hiding the broken vase, covering the stained carpet, and concealing the hole in the wall, you set spotlights on the vase and the hole and move a chair to sit right next to the stain. Your friends arrive and you immediately walk them over to each broken object and stain and begin telling the story of how each happened.

This is a picture of what a believer's life should be. Instead of hiding and pretending to be perfect, we should let our lives be a "Hall of Fails," not the "Hall of Fame."

"Wow, your marriage is so strong!"
"Let me tell you about the three years we hated each other and didn't sleep in the same room."

"You are so full of joy."
"I am now, yes. But let me tell you about the terrible depression I fought from the age of eight to twenty-eight."

"You are so consistent."
"I know. God had to change me because I used to be so addicted to drugs, I couldn't keep any commitments."

"How do you continue to live with hope in such a dark world?"
"When my grandmother passed, it robbed me of so much joy until God gave me a deeper joy than just living this life."

I could go on and on, but let me give you just one more.

"Wow, you wrote God Chose Me. You must be so confident!"
"Oh, let me tell you about my crippling depression and severe anxiety and the time I almost tried to end my marriage and how I never thought I'd be able to have integrity or escape a porn addiction. Let me tell you about how I almost gave up on this book because I lost my memory for three weeks after being hit by a car. Let me tell you how I questioned every word I wrote until I realized it

wasn't me writing but it was God writing through me.
That regardless of my own internal limitation, God Chose
Me."

What you've been through has the potential to be the most powerful part of your testimony. Once you recognize that you are chosen and believe that you are known, accepted, and loved, you have nothing to lose and everything to gain.

Humility: The Path to Your Power

In his beautiful book *Humility of Heart,* Fr. Cajetan Mary da Bergamo wrote, "Humility is the alphabet out of which every other virtue is formed and built up. It is the soil of the garden of the soul, 'the good ground' on which the Divine Sower goes forth to sow His seed."[1]

This is what I want my life to be marked by: an honesty that does not hide my imperfections but brags on them as proof of the goodness of God. An attitude that does not think so highly of myself that I try to maintain some facade of perfection and status. No. May I be so connected to my weakness that when people look at the power and proof in my life, my only response can be, "That could only be God."

No one embraced this posture more than the apostle Paul. In case you're not familiar with him, let me share a little of his backstory.

Saul Is Paul

Saul, who later became known as the apostle Paul, was a devout Pharisee, deeply committed to Jewish law and traditions. (Fun fact: God did not change Saul's name. He was always Paul [see

Acts 13:9]. Paul is simply the Greek name for Saul and the name he went by throughout his ministry. Okay, back to the story.) Saul viewed the early Christian movement, which proclaimed Jesus as the Messiah, as a direct threat to Judaism and the religious order he cherished. Believing he was doing God's will, Saul zealously persecuted Christians, arresting and even approving of their executions, as in the case of Stephen, the first Christian martyr (see Acts 7:58–60).

He did this until his life dramatically changed on the road to Damascus. This is the Paul we encounter in Acts 9:1–18. (I recommend reading this passage if you have time, but I will summarize it here.)

Paul's radical transformation is like a movie. He gets knocked to the ground. Jesus Christ speaks to him. God asks another follower of Jesus, a man named Ananias, to help Saul, the former Christian-killer. And when Ananias questions God's choice of Saul, God says, "Go, for Saul is my *chosen* instrument to take my message to the Gentiles and to kings, as well as to the people of Israel" (Acts 9:15, emphasis mine). God's response is simple: "Ananias, it doesn't matter what you think or feel about Saul's qualifications or past. *I chose him.* Period."

God Chose You, Period

God chose you. Your past does not define you. Your shortcomings are not the limiting factor, and your mistakes are not too big for God to use. Inversely, your successes do not define you either. Your greatest days are not behind you! If you will dare to surrender your plan and path to God, He has something far better for you. He stands ready to bring beauty out of every broken part of your life. He will place you before those who are far more qualified and seem to be the more obvious choice. This is possible when His hand is on you! When you are chosen, your past does not disqualify you; in fact, it is the very thing that equips you for His purpose.

When you recognize the power of God's miraculous grace in choosing you, you gain access to an untouchable confidence. We see glimpses of this confidence throughout Paul's writings. He had a keen awareness that the power and authority he walked in did not come from his pedigree or accomplishments. It was a gift from God that no man can take credit for.

Paul lived a miraculous life for Christ. He went on to plant many churches and wrote over a dozen of the books of the New Testament. One of my favorite letters is Paul's letter to the church of Galatia. He opens the letter by declaring his authority and qualifications to write to them. It's as if his opening chapter is a response to a diss track put out by the other leaders. He basically said in Galatians 1:1, "To be clear, I didn't get this message from any human." This was a direct shot at all the leaders who based their value on the religious leaders they studied under and worked for. He goes on to say what would become the title of this book and the anchor scripture for my life:

Before I was born, God chose me. (Galatians 1:15)

Paul seems to have unlocked something deep in this moment, a confidence deeper than circumstance. He lived with an unapologetic attitude because he knew who chose him and who put him in his position. He found confidence not in the opinions of others but in the fact that he was approved, accepted, and commissioned by the God of the universe. And no one else. When God alone is the source and strength of your confidence, you enter a realm where failures, criticism, and insecurity begin to fade. It's not that they're not there or real. It's just that you have found a better way!

A Better Way

Imagine you are driving with a friend to a location you are familiar with. Maybe it's your favorite restaurant or another friend's house. You know the way like the back of your hand. But as you sit in the passenger seat thinking of the right turn you are about to take, your friend goes straight. "What are you doing? That was our turn!" you shout. Your friend replies that there's a better way, one that is far shorter. You sit there smugly, waiting to prove them wrong—only, you are the one proven wrong. This new path is indeed far quicker than the one you have taken countless times. Sure, the next time you could travel your old route—that old way has not been eliminated. But now you have been enlightened to a better way.

This is what it means to live a "God Chose Me" life. We choose the better way of believing and living as God's chosen children. We do not waste time fighting and getting distracted on the other path. Why? Because that path pales in comparison to the reality that God chose you. On the better path, it doesn't matter what others think or how they define success. Why? Because God chose you. Even your own thoughts and feelings are overshadowed and reshaped by the confidence that you are chosen.

To live with this untouchable confidence is a better way.

All God

My prayer for you is that you would do the exact thing we see Paul doing often in the Scriptures—rooting his identity and worth in his relationship with God through Christ. Too often we derive our value and significance from the comments, perspectives, and opinions of others. The only problem with this process of acquiring confidence is that all these foundations can be shaken.

If you gain your confidence from money, someone will always have more.

If you gain your confidence from winning championships, someone will eventually beat you.

If you gain your confidence from your looks, someone will always be more attractive.

If you gain your confidence from how you are perceived, at some point someone will misunderstand you.

If you gain your confidence from how big your church/house/business is, someone else's will always be bigger.

All of these represent a way you could choose to live. They are just not the *best* way. In fact, not only are they not the best, but they are the most fleeting and insignificant. These sources of confidence do not have the power to uphold the human soul. They are merely a weak foundation that, at some point, is bound to crumble.

I am not saying that others' opinions don't matter; I am saying that they make for a poor foundation for our sense of identity, worth, and purpose. When people begin to question who we are, why we do what we do, or how we walk in such authority, may we point to our creator and say:

"It was God who gave me this gift."

"It was God who called me to start the business."

"It was God who gave me the children and the wisdom to raise them."

"It was God who gave me this idea that is going to change the world."

"It was God who delivered me from the addiction."

"It was God who changed the way I look at myself and allowed me to value my body."

"It was God who chose me."

Before you were even born, there was Someone who fully knew you and fully chose you. He knew everything you would ever do. Every mistake, mishap, and misstep. Every single thing about you that seems broken or insufficient . . . and He still said, "I want you on my team!"

Here's the best part: You didn't have to do anything to earn His choice. He didn't choose you for your looks, your body, your mind, or your muscles. This was before your talent, before your fame, before you had money, before you were an athlete, before you were gifted, before you had received even one compliment. You were chosen for no other reason than that you are *you*.

Take a moment and let that sink in. As the ancient writings say, *Selah*. Pause and think.

You have been chosen not because of your pedigree or performance but simply for the unchanging fact that you are you. Nothing added, nothing taken away. This is grace. A love, a chance, an identity you did not have to ask for but was freely given.

I know that life, family, or circumstance may have told you otherwise. But the truth is, before you were born, you were chosen by the most important person ever. He has never second-guessed His choice and has loved every second of your life. He shines with joy every time you take a breath and stands with infinite excitement every time you start your day. This person thinks about you all the time and looks forward to the day you two finally meet face-to-face. He loves you with an infinite love and has grace for every part of you that feels "wrong." From the beginning of time, He saw you for *you* and said three of the most powerful words in all the universe: *I choose you.*

The God of the universe has chosen you. He has picked you. Selected, identified, called. You are His choice. Not because of anything you could ever do to Him or for Him. (After all, what can we offer an all-powerful, all-knowing, almighty God?) Nevertheless, He overflows with so much love and acceptance for you that He chose you.

With your pain, with your insecurities, with your mistakes. Even with your unbelief that He even exists, He still chose you. The good news of God is this: You don't have to choose Him for Him to choose you.

Security in Sovereignty

In theological circles, there is a concept that I think is extremely important to this conversation. It is known as the sovereignty of God. John Piper said,

> When we say God is sovereign, we mean he is powerful and authoritative to the extent of being able to override all other powers and authorities. That's my effort at a definition. Nothing can successfully stop any act or any event or design or purpose that God intends to certainly bring about. That's my definition.[2]

The sovereignty of God is not some scary, strange concept. Rather, it is *the* greatest source of security and confidence a human can have. The God of the universe has a perfect plan, and this plan includes me being right where I am. If God is all-powerful and His will is perfect, I can have peace knowing that He is working all things out. Romans 8:28 says, "We know that God causes everything to work together for the good of those who love God and are called according to his purpose for them."

This means the confidence I so desperately search for within my own talents, plans, and skills can be replaced with a divine assurance—an untouchable confidence—that God is working things out for me! And not just for me but for His glory and the good of the world.

That is the essence of this book. If you are reading and thinking, *What do you want me to know?* God in His sovereign grace and mercy chooses the most unlikely and underqualified individuals to display His miraculous grace and power. And this power serves as the truest and most steadfast foundation to build a life upon. Because I have been chosen by an all-powerful, all-knowing, almighty God, I can have strength for today.

Chapter 3

THE UNSTOPPABLE MOVEMENT

If their purpose or activity is of human origin, it will fail. But if it is from God, you will not be able to stop these men; you will only find yourselves fighting against God.
—Acts 5:38–39, NIV

U*nstoppable*: impossible to hinder or prevent.

Have you ever known someone who was so dominant in their field they were categorized as unstoppable? Have *you* ever felt unstoppable? I have gradually become an old head when it comes to hooping. However, some friends can testify that this old head can hit a flow no matter which defender you put in front of me. I am shooting and that ball is going in. At that moment, I am unstoppable. Although for me those times may be rare, there are certain athletes who live permanently in this place. Kobe Bryant, the Mamba, with fifteen seconds on the clock: unstoppable. Tom Brady down by a touchdown with one minute on the clock: unstoppable. Tiger Woods down multiple strokes in the 2008 U.S. Open with an injury: unstoppable. My two-year-old, Blue Sunday, when she sees me pour a cup of orange juice for myself and demands, "Dada, ownge juuuizzze": unstoppable. The message of Jesus Christ in the hearts of the first apostles. Unstoppable. The gospel we so often read as a simple story was and still is one of the most radically unstoppable messages in human history. The message of Jesus was so upsetting to the status quo that it sparked immediate backlash and hate. It roused anger to the point of causing the religious leaders to organize a plan to have Jesus executed by the Roman state.

A Message That Must Be Stopped

Jesus's message was perceived to be so dramatic and devastating to the religious system that the Jewish religious leaders of His day decided that the only response was to end this movement by killing its leader. So, they captured Him in the middle of the night and interrogated Him in front of the religious community. They beat Him and mocked Him. They forced Him to drag His own instrument of death to the place He would be killed. They nailed His hands and feet to a cross and watched Him suffocate. The man who had taught thousands, had performed miracles, and had come to bring the kingdom of God to earth had finally been stopped. At least that's what they thought.

Three days later, those who had organized Jesus's murder began to hear rumblings of so-called sightings. But it couldn't be true. The carpenter's son seen walking around alive? Never! They had stopped Him. But the stories grew. The sightings increased into the hundreds. Somehow this man had returned from death. He had beaten the unbeatable. Stopped the unstoppable. How would the religious leaders control this message? How would they contain this movement? To stop the message, they would have to stop His followers.

And this brings us to a pivotal scene in Acts. The early believers had been imprisoned and persecuted for spreading the offensive message that this so-called Savior had risen from the dead. As the apostles were on trial before the religious board, a teacher of the law stepped forward and delivered a compelling argument:

> If their purpose or activity is of human origin, it will fail.
> But if it is from God, you will not be able to stop these men.
> (Acts 5:38–39, NIV)

He knew that if it was merely a human idea, like all human plans it would eventually find its end. However, if God was with these common men—if, in fact, Jesus of Nazareth had risen from the grave and was now empowering these men to preach this message—they would be unstoppable.

WHY I WROTE THIS BOOK

If you've researched this book at all, you may have noticed it's my first. Why is this important? Because the journey has taught me so many valuable lessons about life, hard work, stewarding a dream, and more. Among all the experiences I had while writing this book, one unexpected process I discovered was finding a book while you write it.

For the past ten years, I have written sermons and preached formally and plan to continue doing so. Through this practice, I have discovered a formula that gets me into my rhythm. However, writing a book has been an entirely new journey. Although I had an idea of what this book would be, as I wrote, what emerged was nowhere near the concept that had started as a small seed in my soul. One of the biggest shifts was my target audience. At first, I was trying to write a book that was for both Christians and non-Christians. I love and appreciate many people who do not follow

Jesus, and I did not want my first book to exclude them. But in my desire to be inclusive, I struggled to find the clarity and conviction with which I normally speak.

Although I believe that who I am and the way I live creates a respect and value that will allow this book to reach beyond the traditional Christian faith community, I must be very clear:

My beef is not with atheists; it is with Christians.

What do I mean? Although the message "God Chose Me" can be read by anybody, it is not for everybody. Yes, I hope this message inspires and empowers people wherever they are. But I wrote this book to a specific person.

This book is written to every person who claims to have put their faith in a God who rose from the dead but lives as if He didn't.

So maybe I am talking to you. I am convinced that the worst thing about the Western church is that it is made up of half-committed sellouts to this message of faith. Yes, I said it, and I'm not backing down. We have propagated a message of convenience and low commitment that produces a lackluster life. We skip church, pray inconsistently, and don't read the Bible—or, if we do read it, we put little effort into meditating on it. Instead, we do what we want, when we want. And when we don't get what we want? We blame the church, our pastor, the Bible, and God for the state of our lives.

Friend, I love you enough to be honest with you. A lot of where we are today is our own fault.

Sell Out

If we are honest, many of us have not completely embraced the message of the resurrection. Maybe we experienced a sweet moment at the altar or decided to "give this Jesus thing a try." But I am talking about an all-out, not-afraid-to-look-stupid type of faith. We have settled for the smallest version of the life Jesus calls us to and then have been frustrated with the results. That is not the message of Jesus. His message is not one that can be half-lived. It is a radical message that is marked by dramatic commitment, out-landish faith, and ridiculous risk. The entire foundation of our faith is a Jewish man who was brutally murdered because of the words He said. And many of His closest friends and followers were murdered for believing those words. Jesus's message has been under attack since the moment He entered the world as a baby. But His message has been unstoppable.

Throughout history, governments, leaders, armies, and king-doms have tried to stop this message. But they couldn't. It is unstoppable. These message-bearers have been killed and impris-oned. Fed to the lions. But nothing can stop the message of Jesus Christ.

From its beginning, Christianity has faced intense persecution. In the Roman Empire, emperors like Nero (A.D. 54–68) and Diocle-tian (A.D. 284–305) targeted Christians, blaming them for disasters and forcing them to choose between faith and death. Despite fac-ing cruel methods of death, including crucifixion and being fed to lions, these early Christians did not give in but remained steadfast, their faith often growing stronger in the face of adversity. In more recent history, totalitarian regimes like those under the Soviet Union (1917–91) and communist China have sought to eradicate Christianity, yet the church has endured. In fact, many churches in these areas have grown exponentially in number and in their pas-sionate commitment to Jesus. The Christian faith not only sur-vived these brutal periods but often flourished, spreading to other regions and diversifying in its expression. History has shown that persecution has, paradoxically, galvanized the church, making it resilient and more deeply rooted in the hearts of believers worldwide.

This movement did not consult man, and it does not move at the hand of man. This movement is unstoppable.

WE ARE THE REMNANT

Why is this so important now? Because we are the remnant of this movement. We are the next ones to carry this message. But I'm afraid we have drifted from the boldness of those who came before us. The boldness that led so many women and men to die for this message. The boldness that stirred believers to stand up against evil.

In Acts 5, a claim is made that is just as true today for those who have placed their trust in Jesus: "If they are from God, you will not be able to stop them"(verse 39, my paraphrase). Your faith, your spirit, your confidence should be unstoppable. That is a defining factor of this movement we are a part of—it is unstoppable.

I am not sure under what circumstances you were recruited, but believe me, you are embroiled in a war of eternal significance. It is not a war for earthly possessions but for the human soul. I charge you to live in a manner that reflects the value of this unstoppable movement. To live with courage that does not shy away from confrontation but invites it. To speak with a boldness that is not ashamed to take a stand for the sake of the gospel. To give up comfort and convenience for the cause of Christ. To not just commit but to sell out. If you are going to follow Jesus, then do it with your whole self. His message is far too important and powerful to be watered down by a half-hearted commitment.

To have the untouchable confidence I share about in this book, you must commit to this unstoppable movement.

They are a package deal. A confidence that cannot be moved only comes with the kingdom that cannot be shaken.

It will require a challenging journey to this deep truth. However, as you commit to this process, you'll find yourself leaving the insecurity and inadequacy behind. You will step into a greater reality. One without fear and anxiety. A space where the focus is not on what you are running from but who you are running to. You will discover who you are and why you are here.

We are connected to a long history of faithful followers of Jesus who were so sold out to His cause that they gave their lives for it. This history is far greater than where we stand today. We must remember that among the trials and hardships, one key truth remains: *The movement of Jesus cannot be stopped.*

You are a part of this movement. If you will follow His leading, you, too, shall find yourself in company with our friends in Acts 17:6, "[those] who have turned the world upside down" (ESV).

Chapter 4

HE KNOWS YOU . . . AND HE STILL CHOSE YOU

> *I look up at your macro-skies, dark and enormous,*
> *   your handmade sky-jewelry,*
> *Moon and stars mounted in their settings.*
> *   Then I look at my micro-self and wonder,*
> *Why do you bother with us?*
> *   Why take a second look our way?*
>   —David in Psalm 8:3–4, MSG

The ache in my body, the sensitivity to light, the ringing in my ears. No, I don't have a hangover. I just didn't get a good night's sleep. It's 1 P.M. and I am dead tired. I woke up around 2:30 this morning to catch a direct flight from my tiny airport in Tulsa, Oklahoma, to LAX. Why? Because my friend invited me to be on his podcast. Now, let me be clear—this isn't just any podcast. First, this is a friend who is like family. We share the same "different-ness" that bonds us. He is the creative genius behind some of the most culture-shifting ideas. He also says what he thinks and means what he says—and I like that! Even if it's a little wild. Honestly, that's pretty much true of all my friends. We talk crazy but we believe it. He's a good friend, and his podcast—which he's been doing for some years now with his dad—is awesome. Now, to be 100 percent honest, I'm not sure I would have gotten on a 3:30 A.M. flight to see *just* my friend (maybe a 10:00 A.M.). However, I had the opportunity to sit down with his dad, which meant I was ready to take a paddleboat to LAX if needed. Why? His dad is on my "Freak-Out People" list.

The "Freak-Out People" List

My friends and I have this thing called the "Freak-Out People" list. It's a list of people living or dead who, were you to meet them, would cause you to, well, freak out. I'm not sure how it came up, but while on a road trip to Oklahoma City, we went around and named people on our list. I cannot remember everyone's, but I definitely remember the excitement in my wife's voice when she mentioned Harry Styles. A little *too* excited, in my opinion. (Harry, if you're reading this, we would love to have you over for dinner, but you'll have to sit next to me, not my wife.)

As I went through my list, I first had to consider all the remarkable people I had already met. Many of them are not widely known. In fact, the most special and impactful individuals I've met are known by few. Others, however, you would recognize immediately. After much contemplation, here is my very fluid list. To sum up, my list includes a few specific individuals: Jesus (of course) Brad Pitt, Julia Roberts from the nineties (specifically from *Notting Hill*), Tadej Pogačar, and, as I would soon discover, my friend's dad. I didn't know he was on my list. I realized this about five seconds before I shook his hand for the first time.

I walked into this big auditorium where they record the podcast. I had been in the room before, but this time it was different. I could feel his presence. Not in a weird way, but in the same way you can tell when someone you love or trust walks into the room. A familiar safety. A peace. A presence. A frequency. As I scanned the room, taking in the beauty of the space, he seemed to appear out of thin air. He gently reached out to shake my hand and introduce himself. Then he pulled me in for a hug as if we were old friends. We spoke for a few moments, and then the podcast began. I can't remember where we were in the conversation (I was too busy grasping the fact that he was on my "Freak-Out People" list), but maybe about halfway through, my friend began to tell his dad a bit about who I am and what I do. He looked at my friend, puzzled, and then said something I'll never forget: "I know who he is."

Simple, yes. But to me it was one of the most deeply impactful things he could have said. He went on to share about how he had watched some of my speaking and really appreciated how I communicate. He also asked me some crazy-deep Jedi-type questions that I definitely did *not* answer correctly—but I didn't care! Why? Because one of my heroes *knew me*.[1]

To Be Known

As the 1980s American sitcom *Cheers* theme says,

> *Sometimes you want to go*
> *Where everybody knows your name*
> *And they're always glad you came.*[2]

Everyone wants to be somewhere they are seen, valued, respected, loved, and known. A place where their pain and problems don't disqualify them from fitting in. A place of acceptance, love, encouragement, and grace.

When my friend's dad said, "I know who he is," it struck a chord in my soul that seemed from another dimension. This man was important to me because of the impact he had on my life. I had watched countless hours of his speaking, read his books, and watched his interviews. As much as I possibly could, I knew him.

But this was different. I didn't just know him. *He knew me.*

It's Not Who You Know but Who Knows You

I've heard it said, "It's not *what* you know, it's *who* you know."

I believe that to be true, but I think it could be better stated, "It's not *who* you know, it's *who knows you.*" I mean, think about it. If you walk into a Drake, Beyoncé, or Taylor Swift concert, climb all the way down the bleachers, step onto the floor, stroll up to the front, and try to walk backstage, you will, of course, be stopped by some bald, angry-looking guy in a shirt that says **SECURITY**. Imagine saying, "Let me through, I know [Drake, Beyoncé, Taylor]." This could go a lot of ways, but let me guarantee you, that guy does not give two rips about who *you* know. Why? You may know [Drake, Beyoncé, Taylor], but [Drake, Beyoncé, Taylor] does not know you.

But now imagine you are stuck in this moment and [Drake, Beyoncé, Taylor] yells from backstage, "Hey, let them through. I know them!" You, of course, shrug nonchalantly and walk by with a little swag, staring down the security guard who tried to hold you back.

It is not just about who you know. The true value is in who knows you. I say all of this to make one simple yet definitive point.

God Knows Who You Are

Depending on your current relationship status with God, this might feel like old news, new news, or bad news. But let me be clear: This is nothing but *great* news for you and me.

God. Yahweh. Jehovah. Creator of the heavens and the earth. The One who was, who is, and who will always be. Who the book of Revelation says is coming back with tattooed thighs and riding a white unicorn. (Okay, it doesn't say the unicorn thing and I'm not sure about the tattoo, but I have a theory both are possible. See 19:6) Anyway, *God*. King of kings and Lord of lords. The God of Abraham, Isaac, and Jacob. Who split the Red Sea and rained fire from heaven for Elijah. *That* God. He stands from age to age. As the Reverend Dr. S. M. Lockridge famously preached:

> He heals the sick . . .
> He forgives sinners . . .
> He's the pathway of peace
> He's the roadway of righteousness
> He's the highway of holiness
> He's the gateway of glory . . .
> Death couldn't handle Him
> And the grave couldn't hold Him
> That's my King!
> He always has been
> And He always will be[3]

When I consider all His grandness, all His knowledge, wisdom, and power, I find myself remembering the passage I shared at the beginning of this chapter and resonating with the words of David, which are worth reading again:

> I look up at your macro-skies, dark and enormous,
>   your handmade sky-jewelry,
> Moon and stars mounted in their settings.
>   Then I look at my micro-self and wonder,
> Why do you bother with us?
>   Why take a second look our way? (Psalm 8:3–4, MSG)

I'm not sure where David was when he wrote those words. We know he had a roller coaster of a life. Giants, betrayal, rejection from his own family, deep-seated trauma, and public moral failure. David was no stranger to rejection or brokenness. Perhaps from this place he began to ponder the reality that the God who led his forefathers to the promised land had also trained His eye on him. That somehow, in all of God's infinite to-do list for the universe, He remained mindful of David: what his needs were, what fears and insecurities he struggled with. Somehow the God of the universe had enough time, space, and energy to be mindful of him.

Friend, I have good news for you. This reality was not only true for David in 980 B.C.; it rings true for you and me today. God, the creator of the universe, knows who you are. The Scriptures go so far as to say He knows the number of hairs on our heads (see Matthew 10:30). This thought alone should spark our hearts with wonder, gratitude, and joy. *The God of the universe knows who I am.*

But as amazing as this is, it's not even the best part. The greatest reality is not that God knows you but that He fully knows you *and He still chose you.* Why is this such significant news? Because usually the knowledge of someone's shortcomings gives warrant to avoid choice rather than invoke choice.

COMPLICATED CHOICES

Have you ever had to pick teams when you didn't know who you were playing with? Let's say you are playing basketball, and you are chosen as captain. What do you do? You start judging *everyone.* You first look around for someone tall and think back on who you saw make a shot while you were warming up. If you're really skilled at picking, you wait a while before choosing. Why? Because the real hoopers are like my friend Michiah. On any given Monday night in Tulsa, he will be on the sideline having walked in twenty minutes late and still sitting in his slides. He couldn't care less about a warm-up because he was born warmed up. These types of people are annoyingly good. They came out of the womb with a jumper and can decide to go off at will. They are the people who usually get picked first because, well, they don't suck—and your choice of someone is always influenced by your knowledge of them.

So if you are tasked with choosing a team and you have no knowledge of the players, you will always be at a disadvantage. Why is this important? Because you are trying to win, and some people . . . well, some people are trash at basketball. It's just that simple. They were dealt cards in life and none of those cards point to them being picked for my team.

Often, our choices are simplified or complicated based on past relationships. If we know someone is not faithful, we are not likely to enter a high-pressure situation with them. If we know someone to be unkind, we are unlikely to share our deepest fears. If someone has been untruthful, we would rarely trust their word for direction. Whether we admit it or not, we judge people by their past to help determine our interaction with them in the future. But God is not like that.

Think about it. We are inconsistent, we don't commit, we fail, we lie, we do all the things God asks us not to do. But for some reason, He still chooses us. He still chose me. He still chose you.

What am I saying? God knows you best. He knows you inside and out. He knows your future and your past, your strengths and weaknesses. He knows that you have broken your word countless times. He knows the things you don't share with anyone. He knows the bad things in your head and heart. He knows everything about you and He still chose you. This is the point where, if you were at church with me, my friend Rosevelt would break into spontaneous song, yelling, "Yes, I still got a reason!" and the room would erupt into a praise break. God knows my mess and He chose me anyway!

If They Knew the Real Me

To be fully loved, you must first be fully known. In fact, I would say that it is almost impossible to love someone completely until you know them fully—the best and the worst parts. The truth is, for most of my life I lived in the category of "If they knew the real me."

> If They Really Knew . . .
>
> my struggle . . .
>
> what I thought about . . .
>
> what happened to me when I was a child . . .
>
> my secrets . . .
>
> what I think about at night . . .
>
> I am a fraud . . .
>
> I am afraid . . .

We worry that if others found out the truest things about us, it would somehow cancel out any good we have to offer.

God really knows and He hasn't moved a step. In fact, the Bible says it is our weakness and brokenness that draw Him close. Psalm 34:18 says, "The LORD is close to the brokenhearted; he rescues those whose spirits are crushed."

God has chosen you not despite knowing you but *because* He

knows you. He knows you better than you know yourself. He knows that who you think you are is far from the fullest picture of who you *truly* are. He knows you so well He believes not in your worst habits but in your greatest potential. God knows you and He still chose you.

This understanding waters our soul with the love and acceptance we need to grow a life of beauty and confidence. You do not have to hide or change to receive love. And when you know this, it changes you.

You begin trusting the beauty on the inside of you and stepping into everything with a grand conviction that you matter. You have something vital to offer the world. To be fully known and fully loved releases the human soul from its cage of fear and insecurity. When we believe we are truly known and loved, our souls can soar to heights previously unseen. When we realize we are seen by God, the acknowledgment of others may still matter; however, it is not as powerful over our egos or insecurities. We can live with a confidence than cannot be tainted by the world because it is the gift of a divine God.

My friend, the God of the universe knows you *and* He chose you.

This changes everything.

It's one thing to hear it, but it's another to believe it and live like it's true.

Chapter 5

THE REJECT EFFECT

Selected or marked for favor or special privilege.
—*Definition of "Chosen" in* Merriam-Webster Dictionary

"All right, everyone line up!" yells the PE teacher. "Zach, who's your first pick?" Your heart starts to race, your palms get sweaty, and every insecurity you've ever had floods your mind. It's every sixth grader's worst nightmare: picking teams for a game of kickball.

"Uhh, let's see . . . Sarah."

"Jason."

"Sam."

"Caleb"

"Emily . . ."

Your name isn't anywhere on the horizon. Then it happens. You look around and your worst fear is unfolding before your eyes: It's just you and one other person. Suddenly, any care or concern for the other kid goes out the window and you pray one of the most honest prayers of your life. *God, if You could please let me not be picked last, I would really appreciate it.* What could be worse than being picked last in PE? The embarrassment, the humiliation. Nothing could be worse than this very moment.

Okay, pause. Was it just me or did this scene transport you back through time into that awkward sixth-grade body waiting to be rejected? No matter where you were raised, how popular you were, or how many talents you possessed, we all had a moment like that.

Your First Rejection

In an incredible sermon titled "The Disease of Double-Minded," my friend Mike Todd made this powerful statement: "You cannot heal from a diagnosis you do not understand."[1] In that same spirit, I think it's vitally important to understand the impact that rejection has had on our lives before we try to run with this untouchable confidence. You cannot skip over the scars of your past in order to get to your desired outcome. You must work through it. Whether we admit it or not, all of us have experienced some form of rejection that has affected our ability to walk in confidence.

It may not have been a game of kickball. Maybe it was your first crush—you put yourself out there only to be shot down in front of your friends.

Or perhaps you walked in late to the lunchroom and didn't have anywhere to sit and no one moved over.

Or maybe you worked extremely hard throughout high school to ensure your acceptance to the college of your dreams—even taking extra courses and unpaid internships to boost your application—only to get the same rejection letter as everyone else.

Maybe it was getting passed over for your dream job or long-awaited promotion. You worked harder than anyone, but the boss didn't see your value and chose someone else.

Perhaps a lifelong friend swore they would never leave, but one thing led to another and now you can't remember the last time they texted back.

Maybe it was more than just a friend—your mother or father. They were supposed to be the one person who would never walk out on you. But at way too young an age, you found yourself navigating life without them.

Your spouse, the love of your life. You vowed to love each other in sickness and health, but suddenly, after three kids and twenty years of marriage, they were unfaithful.

I'm not sure what that moment is for you, but take a moment and think back. What was the first or most impactful rejection? Even though the news or media often tells us otherwise, we have far more that unites us than separates us. We *all* have experienced the deep pain of rejection.

REJECTION REWIRES

Rejection hurts in the moment, but it also wires our brains for the future. Mark Leary, a neuroscientist at Duke University, reported that "people not only react strongly when they perceive that others have rejected them, but a great deal of human behavior is influenced by the desire to avoid rejection."[2] In other words, a lot of our actions, thoughts, what we do and don't do are simply an attempt not to be rejected ever again.

Dr. Leary's research shows the massive impact rejection has on every human being down to the neurological level, whether on the basketball court or in the boardroom, on the playground or the platform. We have all experienced the gut-wrenching effects of rejection—not only in that moment but also long after the fact. We take the seeds of rejection and adjust our behavior, personality, and even our most central characteristics simply to avoid the burning shame of being rejected. We do this as a defense mechanism. Our bodies remember the pain of our last rejection and say, "Ain't no way we're doing that again." So we change. We adapt. We transform. I wish I could say it's all for the better, but many (most) times it's not. We end up changing some of the most valuable parts of who we are. Why on earth would that feel like a good idea?

Because the pain of someone else's rejection isn't so bad if *you've* already rejected you.

The Green Machine

Imagine it's your first day of school and you are *ready*. You stayed up all night prepping. You triple-checked that you have all your supplies: backpack, pencils, lined paper, Trapper Keeper (yes, I'm that old). Most importantly, you have carefully laid out your first-day-of-school outfit. Every stitch of every piece of clothing is green because over the summer you decided green is your favorite color. Green is everything. Green is life. Green is the color of your soul.

Your mom, kind and gracious as she is, used all her Kohl's Cash to buy you a whole new wardrobe—all green. From your head to your toes, you look like a piece of edamame, and you are proud. You wake up early, get dressed, eat breakfast, and are out the door at 7:15 A.M. sharp, more than ready to take on your first day.

You get to school and head inside. You have about ten minutes before school starts, which is perfect—just enough time to show off your outfit before first period. You see your friends gathered in a circle and run up with a big smile on your face, and just as you are about to brag about your new threads, someone stops you in your tracks. "Guys, who invited the green bean to school?" Everyone busts out laughing. You try to shake it off (okay, it *was* a good joke). "But for real, who would ever wear that? It looks dumb! Come on guys, let's go!"

You stand there in shock. You wander to your locker and then to your first class. You sit through the whole day with their words on repeat in your mind. You *finally* make it home and your mom asks, "Sweetie, how was your first day?"

"Fine," you say as walk straight to your room.

Opening your closet door, you see it: green. Everything is green. Your shoes, your shirts, your pants, *everything*. It's all green, your new favorite color. Well . . . it *was* your favorite. Because as much as you loved green, there's a problem.

You look dumb in green . . . at least that's what everyone else thinks.

This story might seem silly, but it illustrates a key point and leads me to ask, What is your green? What did you love that seemed to make it hard for others to love you?

Your "Green Moment"

We all have our "green moment," the moment we realized we didn't fit. When we knew there was something slightly *off* about us. Maybe for you it was external: height, weight, eye color, hair type, skin. Or maybe it felt far more personal, more connected to the inner you. Your brain, your personality, your heart, your soul. Just *you*.

It's the moment you began to believe that something in you is broken. Everyone but you seems to have it together.

Other moms have time for their husband, hobbies, working out, taking care of the kids, and posting about it on Instagram. But you—it took everything you had just to get out of bed today.

Other couples don't argue. They take trips and travel the world together. Not y'all, though. You haven't had a night out in God knows how long, and once the kids are out of the house you will basically be strangers.

Everyone else seems to have it together with their money. They save, spend, and give in perfect proportions. Never stressed, never worried. Meanwhile, you are filled with the deepest anxiety as the bills and credit card interest continue to pile up. Your phone rings off the hook with collectors, and there's nothing you can do to get ahead.

No one you talk to seems to struggle with porn. They all outgrew it, moved past it, or just gave it up. But you? You can't fall asleep without it. The shame haunts you and you walk around feeling so empty it's hard to look people in the eyes.

Other people don't question their faith. They are always quick to trust God and seem to have more hope than you. All you've got is questions. Questions the pastor isn't answering and, if you're honest, you're scared to ask.

You feel confused, worried, and afraid to even question who you are or who you have to become. Everyone else seems to know who they are and what they want to be. You look in the mirror and barely recognize who you see. The problem must be you. Something is missing.

So what do you do?

Change, of course.

If who you are isn't enough, change. Become someone who is better, different, worth it.

No matter how big or small your rejection was, it planted a seed—and every seed planted in fertile soil produces fruit. Through countless conversations, counseling sessions, and experiences, I have found this to be true.

The seed of rejection in the soil of insecurity always produces the fruit of the fake you.

THE PAIN OF SELF-REJECTION

Now, before we go any further, I have to address a group of individuals who may have found that last section hard to relate to. Maybe you have not experienced any traumatic external rejections. Maybe you have moved on from the jokes and insults from your classmates. Maybe you have made it past the rejection of others. But the truth is, there is a rejection that cuts far deeper than that. It is the pain of self-rejection.

The rejection seed can even be cast by someone else, even someone who doesn't know you or care about you. They may overlook your superpower and see only what the surface has to offer. However, there is a deep pain and slow fade that come with rejecting a portion of ourselves. It's not always obvious. So sometimes the rejection doesn't even stem from within ourselves; oftentimes we take the seeds or statements of others and grow our own garden of disappointment.

What started as a small thought, we now water with our insecurities and experiences. We reinforce it with our negative self-talk, and before long we have completely manipulated our mind into the darkest and most unsafe place. We constantly tear ourselves down. We remind ourselves how unqualified and unimportant we are. If we are honest, the issue does not lie in the pain of what others have said but in what we have allowed to grow. And when we give space to these negative thoughts and emotions, there's always a cost.

How Much Did Rejection Cost You?

What would you do to be accepted by others? Better yet, what have you already done? What have you changed about yourself, what lies have you told, what stories have you believed, what beauty have you suppressed in hopes of avoiding that feeling of being rejected? What parts of you have been locked away to avoid the pain, fear, and failure of being rejected.

It's okay to be honest. There's no judgment and no pressure.

Maybe you have gradually stopped speaking up because your ideas are usually met with weird looks and don't seem to catch on.

Perhaps you have stopped being honest about your desires because you don't want to be a burden. You've settled for surface relationships and have given up hope of ever finding real love because trust feels too risky.

Maybe you haven't pursued the job or career you've always wanted because of one failure in your past. It was a moment, but now that moment has become all you see.

Maybe you shyly keep to the background, not because it is natural or what you desire, but because somewhere along the way you accepted that you were not important or valuable enough to be heard or seen.

Maybe you stopped being your authentic self, engaging in code-switching depending on which friends are around. You talk one way at work and another at home. You dress one way during the week and another on the weekend.

Perhaps the idea of being rejected by your family has kept you in the same place, the same city, for years. It's now at the point where you have begun to resent the very place you find yourself in.

What have you done to avoid rejection?

What has it cost you?

Whatever your answer, the price is too high. You are far too important, far too valuable, far too special to sacrifice any bit of your uniqueness, your beauty, or your power to gain others' acceptance. I don't care who they are—a parent, coach, significant other, boss, mentor, pastor, celebrity, aunt, or uncle. There is no human on this earth that is worth you suppressing the best parts of yourself. No one.

Let me stop for a moment and clarify what I am *not* saying. I am not saying the classic yearbook message, "Never change"—which is some of the worst advice you could ever receive. Can you imagine if you never changed after ninth grade? My goodness. I'm embarrassed just thinking about what I'd be wearing right now. Growth is an essential part of the human experience. We are all meant to grow and become.

However, you were *not* meant to suppress parts of yourself for the sake of acceptance. You were not made to hold back who you really are out of fear of what people might think, say, or do. *Absolutely not.*

You Are Worth So Much More

Do not settle.

Do not sacrifice.

Do not step back.

Do not change just so they will call you back.

Do not sacrifice what you know is right just so they will give you the job.

Do not stop doing what you love just because your family doesn't understand.

Do not do something you hate simply to feel seen.

Do not give away the most precious parts of yourself for a cheap moment of pleasure. You deserve far more than that. You are worth someone's complete time and attention. You are worth being claimed in public. You are worth being seen and valued for the unique gifts you bring to the table. You are worth someone's investment and commitment.

Flaws and all, *you are special.*

So where was it? When was your first rejection? How did it happen? But most importantly, how did it make you feel? I ask because, to plant something new, you must first identify and uproot what's already growing there—and in some cases, you must completely change the soil.

The Soil of Your Soul

I did not grow up on a farm or with a garden, but my grandfather (Poppie) and late grandmother (Mimi) owned a flower shop for over thirty years called Ted & Debbie's. Mimi and Poppie taught me many valuable lessons, but one that stands out is the importance of soil. No matter how beautiful the plant is, no matter how good it looks when you leave the store, if you do not plant it in the right soil and give it the right attention, it will not last.

Our souls and lives are similar. I can give you all the tips and tricks to be confident. We can discuss the amazing life that stands in front of you, but if you do not allow God to replace the soil of your heart, you will never be able to grow.

Rejection Was Never Written

The reason rejection cuts us at such a deep level is that it was never a part of the plan. It goes against the core truth of the human soul.

Somewhere deep down, we know we deserve to be accepted. We know we should be loved and cared for—and not for what we do but simply for who we are.

We have all witnessed injustice or unkindness toward another human, and when we do, something rages inside us. No matter our race, religion, or gender, we all have a sense that there's meant to be a general acceptance and basic respect for simply being alive. Even if we don't always get it, we know we deserve it.

We were never supposed to experience rejection.

It was not in our original script to feel the pain of being overlooked, misused, or neglected.

We were created to be fully loved, fully accepted, and fully cared for.

We were created to be seen, valued, and loved.

We were created to be chosen.

GOD REALLY DID CHOOSE YOU

It is my deepest conviction that this revelation has the potential to radically shift your life. There are a few Mount Rushmore moments in life: when you choose the god you will serve, the person you will marry, the purpose or pursuit you will dedicate your life to. And right up there with those moments, I believe, is grasping the reality that *God chose you.* If you can comprehend this, your life stands ready to shine like the most beautiful sunrise. Full of potential, excitement, and hope. There is a confidence that you can hold on to and never lose. It does not have to waver based on your performance. It does not have to shift with the wind of appreciation or criticism you receive from others. It is secured deep inside you—in a space only you and God have access to.

My friend, God really did choose you. He loves you and He has an incredible life awaiting you. My challenge, your challenge, our challenge is to truly accept and believe this fact. You may have experienced the effects of rejection in ways that my writing cannot begin to articulate or acknowledge. It may have cost you years of your life. And yet the greatest reality is, though you may have been rejected by people, you are totally accepted by God.

You do not have to live in the aftermath of your rejection. You do not have to remain a victim of others' words. You do not have to continue to shy away from who you are supposed to be. You do not have to lessen yourself just to stay in that relationship. Today you can make one of the greatest decisions of your life. You can turn the page on a new day and a new you. You can step out from the pain of rejection and into the light of a new beginning. You can step into a life where you are not defined by the words of others but by the grace and word of God over your life. In fact, I urge you to move forward. Leave those hurtful words and that rejection behind. What are you waiting for? You know what God has placed inside of you, yet you have let others' comments or your own fear keep you stuck. No longer! It is time to move on and move forward! *You may have experienced rejection, but you are not rejected.* You are completely and wholly accepted by God.

It may take time, effort, counseling, confession, and even more time. But I believe that we *can* accept and own this truth in the depths of our soul. And when we do . . . everything changes. In this very moment, we are making the choices to take our power back. No longer will the words of others or ourselves rob us of the future we dream of!

So, for maybe the first time in your life, I want you to say this. Out loud, under your breath, or maybe just in your head because you don't want people to look at you weird. However you choose to do it, do it. Repeat after me.

God.

Chose.

Me.

Chapter 6

A SINGULAR SYMPHONY

The perfect orchestration of the symphony of life is one of the Creator's greatest and most beautiful miracles.
    —*Suzy Kassem*, Rise Up and Salute the Sun

Here is something you might not know about me: I love classical music. The works listed below are considered to be some of the most iconic and incredible symphonies ever composed:

Beethoven's Symphony No. 5

Beethoven's Symphony No. 9 in D Minor, Op. 125 "Choral"

Bagatelle No. 25 in A Minor, WoO 59 "Für Elise"

Mozart's Symphony No. 41 in C Major, K. 551 "Jupiter"

Berlioz's Symphonie fantastique, Op. 14, H. 48

Nocturne in E-flat Major, Op. 9, No 2

If you're not familiar with classical music, I highly encourage you to listen to these. A symphony is the beauty, artistry, and wonder of many individuals working together to create one beautiful display of art and musicianship. These groups can be arranged in an almost infinite number of ways with a seemingly infinite number of musicians. According to an article on the official Guinness World Records site, "The largest orchestra consists of 8,573 musicians and was achieved by El Sistema Nacional de Orquestas y Coros Juveniles e Infantiles de Venezuela (Venezuela), in Caracas, Venezuela, on 13 November 2021."[1]

In fact, as I write this chapter, I am listening to a playlist of the greatest symphonies ever composed. The best symphonies find their power in juxtaposition—the beauty of multiple parts coming together to express one sound. Each musician must find his or her position, and it is only in the humility and submission to these positions that the fullness of beauty can be displayed. Each instrument must show up fully and completely, for without one part the whole cannot be. The beauty of singularity and yet the power of unity are simultaneously displayed.

Now, I wish I could say I was using the symphony as an analogy to display the beauty I feel on the inside. However, many times my soul has felt like an out-of-tune and out-of-time orchestra that cannot find the same note. It feels like every instrument is fighting for a solo or simply lacking direction. It has been and will continue to be the journey of my life to fine-tune this orchestra to playing the music God has written for my life.

If you ever take the time to listen to an orchestra performing an incredibly composed symphony, it can often be somewhat jarring. The wind instruments are playing a soft solo and then the drums and cymbals crash in out of nowhere. Then comes some weird instrument you've never heard of spiraling out of control. Not to mention the random opera singer who is belting out words none of us recognize. To be honest, there is nothing that could better articulate the inside of my mind and soul.

The beauty and complexity of an orchestra perfectly depicts the reality of every individual on this planet. We often live as though we are truly singular individuals. We buy into the idea that we are one-sided people with little depth. We do our thing and that is it. But deep down, we know this could not be further from the truth. We are complex individuals with many different facets and talents. We carry the complexity and beauty of God in our very makeup.

ONE GOD, THREE PERSONS

Take a moment and "consider the rock from which you were cut," as Isaiah 51:1 states. Then let's navigate some theological waters. Our God, whom I wholeheartedly believe we each reflect in our very DNA, is not just a singular, basic God. He is one God in three persons. This idea in Scripture is called the Trinity. He is singular in that He is not three separate gods. However, at the same time He is three different persons in God the Father, God the Son, and God the Holy Spirit. Each of these persons of God is displayed and identified throughout the Old and New Testaments. They are all God and all serve a very specific role in our lives.

THE TRINITY (THE OG BIG THREE)

God the Father is our creator. He is a good Father who created this world and developed the greatest rescue mission of all time by sending His Son when we desperately needed rescuing.

God the Son, or Jesus Christ, is our savior. He paid the price we could not pay. He was the only one who could pay the debt that our sin racked up with God. Without Him we are left to our own performance and good works—which basically means we are screwed.

God the Holy Spirit is our helper. He is the promise that was sent to earth to help us as we navigate this world. He is often described as a "feeling" or "something told me," but He is a person who is our advocate and power.

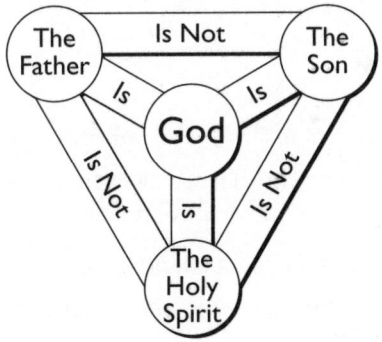

They are all God and all different yet all equal. Now, if God is triune in nature and we are made in the image of God, what does that mean for you and me? I think it means there is more than one side to us, and we must learn to operate as a singular symphony.

MAN OF MANY HATS

As I was working to develop the art for my book, I became stuck. Not for a lack of ideas, but for a lack of clarity and connection. I kept asking myself, which idea would communicate the heart of this message? Through some amazing collaboration we landed on this idea of doing a photoshoot displaying all the different sides of me. So, on the back of the book, there are several different photos that represent a story or a part of me.

To illustrate further, I want to comment briefly on each of the photos. (If you are reading the ebook, you can find the back cover online.)

> *Underneath the Desk*—This is the weak and broken Charles. All of us have parts that we try to hide. That man under the desk is vulnerable and weak, rippled with anxiety, suicidal thoughts, and the pressures of life. He is definitely not the obvious person to be chosen by God.

> *The Denim and Bolo Tie*—This photo represents my childhood in Bowling Green, Kentucky. Kentucky is my foundation. A lot of my core memories originate in BG. Kentucky holds a blend of experiences, from my hardest laughs to some of my toughest pains. It represents all our origin stories—the parts of our pasts we cherish and those we wish we could change. It is the mixed bag that is all our family of origin. It is beauty and the brokenness that comes from my childhood and includes my alter ego, "Kentucky Cowboy."

> *Me and My Wild Chickens*—Here I am being a dad, trying his best to pass along only the best aspects of our family. It is equal parts fun and frustrating, with the pressure of trying to "do it right." To live, laugh, and love well.

> *Me and My Wife*—I am a husband who feels the burden to create a marriage where his wife feels loved and safe. I also carry the burden of being a broken man. My saf-

est place is being with her. The commitment and risk of putting all of your love into one person.

Me and My Son in Allen Iverson Jerseys—In this photo my son is wearing my childhood Allen Iverson jersey. Iverson was and still is my favorite player of all time. He was the first version of confidence I saw that made me want to walk with my head held high. It is the pieces of me that I love, and it has served me well.

The Leather Jacket—The jacket in this photo is not just any leather jacket. It is the jacket of hero-turned-best-friend Carl Lentz. He is the reason I felt like I could do ministry and is one of the people I call during my most challenging moments. This represents the journey from watching those who have gone before you to owning your moment. Being confident that this is your time.

There are a few other photos mixed in that represent the other pieces of me. Family man, pastor, creative, Jesus-follower, son, and more. Each of these photos is significant because it represents a different part that makes me, me. They are all different, yet they are all me!

MORE THAN JUST A . . .

The reason I included these photos is not to show off my wife, kids, and cool fits. However, my wife is gorgeous, my kids are beautiful, and my fits go crazy. The real reason is to communicate through art what I believe to be an essential truth: We are all made up of many parts. No matter how people label us, we can never be narrowly defined as one thing. We are many things to many people. We carry responsibilities, stories, and purpose in different ways. As we grow and mature, we slowly find other parts of us. It happens naturally. We start out very simply as children, but as life goes on, we slowly find ourselves switching between the multiple hats and responsibilities we carry.

As we continue to grow and change, however, we may find ourselves stuck in certain roles with certain people. We feel stuck being *just* a mother or *just* a friend or *just* a worker.

Perhaps at work you are the numbers guy, at home you are the fixer, with the guys you are the casual one, on Fridays you are the family man, and on the inside you are unsure of everything.

Or maybe your friends know you as the wild one, your family knows you as the successful daughter, your boyfriend knows you as the loving girlfriend, and your mom knows you as the distant child. However, on the inside there seems to be less and less space to keep adding these different parts. Slowly the pressure begins to build. You find yourself forgetting who you are when you're around certain people.

As I navigate the pressures involved in each of my roles, I consistently ask myself the same question: Will anyone accept all of me? If I stopped switching and pretending and was just me—all of me—what would happen? Would that work? If you have been brave enough to attempt this feat, it may have left you feeling defeated and even confused. For me it has always landed me at some version of "There is probably no one who would or can accept all of me."

And that brings us to the truth and purpose of this book as we answer the question, Is there anyone who would ever accept or choose all of me?

God Chose All of You

You were created not only to be chosen but also to be fully accepted. When God created this earth, He placed humans in an environment that was designed and designated for their flourishing. In the beauty of His plan, humans had no need to prove themselves or work for acceptance. There was no impressing others with their smarts or talents. They didn't have to show their worth through their accomplishments or financial status. God's command to Adam and Eve to "tend and watch over" the garden (Genesis 2:15) was an invitation to join God in cultivating Eden for their flourishing. They did not earn God's love and acceptance through their work—they already possessed God's love and acceptance simply by being made in God's image (see Genesis 1:27). God told Jeremiah, "I chose you before I gave you life, and before you were born I selected you to be a prophet to the nations" (Jeremiah 1:5, GNT). Before the fall, humans worked out of love for God and from a position of acceptance. It was only after the lie of the devil that we traded simply being with God for trying to prove our worth through our work. And from that moment forward, humanity has been striving, working, scratching, clawing for someone—*anyone*—to see and accept us.

A Love like Notting Hill

As you learned earlier, I may or may not have a slight crush on nineties Julia Roberts. Okay, honestly a massive crush! This all stems from one of my and my wife's all-time favorite movies, *Notting Hill*. Will (played by Hugh Grant) is the owner of a small bookstore in London. One day, the most famous actress in the world,

Anna Scott (Julia Roberts), walks into the store. Will and Anna eventually fall in love, but because of the complications of her fame and celebrity life, they don't seem able to make it work. In a last-ditch effort, Anna unexpectedly shows up at the bookstore and asks if there is any way Will might reconsider their relationship. Against his own feelings and desires, Will rejects her offer. He is too scared that it will not work because of who she is.

It is at this moment that Julia Roberts says one of the most vulnerable, heartrending lines in film history. With tears in her eyes, she lays it all on the line for love:

"I'm also just a girl, standing in front of a boy, asking him to love her."

You may not find yourself in a London-based nineties rom-com, but this sentence is true for all of us. More than we want the date, the job, the friend circle—more than anything—we just want to know that someone would love us. That someone would accept us for who we really are. That they would see all our imperfections, our hurdles, and still choose to love us.

That we would be chosen.

I Am Sorry You Weren't Accepted

I'm not sure where you are on your journey of acceptance, but wherever it is, I want to say three words you may have yet to hear:

I am sorry.

I am sorry you were not accepted. I am sorry others did not acknowledge the infinite beauty, strength, and uniqueness you carry. I am sorry you felt the pain of disapproval. I am sorry others did not protect you as they should have.

The pain this caused you was never supposed to be the plan for you. The deep pain of being overlooked, undervalued, and ultimately rejected was never supposed to grace the innermost parts of who you are.

As much as life has told you that you are only accepted in part, there is a God who fully accepts you. The broken and the best parts. The part of you with answers and the part with questions. He does not expect you to be anything but yourself. He accepts you as you are and where you are.

It is with this understanding and truth that the power of an untouchable confidence begins to take root in your soul. When you begin to embrace that you are chosen, you will find access to your "bag."

GET IN YOUR BAG

As you can probably tell, I like to make basketball references. Sorry, not sorry. I was raised watching AND1 mixtape videos and perfecting my crossover on a bumpy driveway. Anyway, there is a term in basketball called a *bag*. It can be used many ways, but generally it refers to a player's set of go-to moves that allow them to get open and help them score. Over the years, I have had to adjust my bag. My primary bag consists of hard jab steps, full-speed cuts across the floor, and a one-step fadeaway across the right top of the key.

How does this relate to our untouchable confidence? No matter what others have said or how much they judge you, *get in your bag.* I don't know what your go-to moves are, but I am confident that God has placed something special inside you. When you begin to second-guess your shot, you are not at your best. It is only when you use what you have that God will fully express His power in you.

If your thing is encouragement, get in your bag.

If your thing is cooking, get in your bag.

If your thing is making epic TikToks, get in your bag.

If your thing is raising kids to be great humans, get in your bag.

If your thing is teaching on a very specific theory, get in your bag.

If your thing is being a theological samurai, get in your bag.

If your thing is _____, get in your bag.

Now, I must pause to clear up something both practical and theological. I am not saying, "Hey, God accepts you, so do whatever you want." *Absolutely not.* There are parts of us that are twisted, broken, sinful, and outright evil. These are the parts that Scripture calls our "flesh" (see Galatians 5 and Romans 7) and are enemies of God. God loves us as we are but refuses to leave us as we are. He loves us to transform us. To mold us into the version of ourselves we so desperately desire to become.

You Are a Masterful Singular Symphony

What am I saying, then? You are a divine symphony. You are many beautiful parts that all deserve to be expressed in the right tune and tone. Perhaps life has convinced you that there aren't many people who would fully love you if they fully knew you—but God is the one person who can accept all of you. And when you surrender to Him, He stands ready to take your out-of-control orchestra and bring it together to perform some of the greatest music that would speak to the goodness and glory of God.

As you surrender to God as the conductor of your life, this surrender not only changes you but also releases those around you. I have witnessed this in the life of my best friend Mike. Someone once asked me what I thought Mike's superpower was and I said, "The reason older white ladies and almost every other socioeconomic group and race come to hear Mike speak is not because they have *so* much in common. It is because he is so himself that he gives others the power to be themselves." This is my prayer for you. That as you embrace your divine design, it would produce an extreme confidence on the inside of you that would free not only you but those around you.

I pray for the parents reading this book, that your children would be raised by a mother or father who knows their worth. That your friends would know what it is to experience only encouragement and never judgment. That the ones who are closest to you would be freed to truly be their God-created selves because there is someone like you in their lives.

May the revelation "God Chose Me" free you to live your music loudly. May the beauty of the notes of your life echo in eternity. May you increasingly realize you are an image bearer of our triune God who has commissioned you to express the divine beauty of God through all your talents, quirks, and qualities. Just as God has multiple facets to His grandness, so, too, were you meant to reflect His beauty in multiple ways.

Be Both

Do not settle into the lie that you can only be one thing. That you have only one note to be played. Never listen to those who are afraid to play their instruments. Play yours and play loud.

All of you deserves a spot at the table.

> If you are a mother and a successful businesswoman, be both.

> If you are a compassionate father and a strong-willed man, be both.

> If you are an artist and an athlete, be both.

> If you are a business owner and a servant, be both.

> If you are a pastor and a music producer, be both.

> If you are a student of medicine and a gamer, be both.

> If you are an international superstar and a devoted family man, be both.

> If you are a barber and a counselor, be both.

> If you are a designer and a dad, be both.

> If you are of mixed race, be both.

> If you are single and you are someone who desires marriage, you can be both—you can honor God in your singleness while still seeking someone to spend your life with.

Too often we let others pressure us into shrinking into a box rather than growing into who God has called us to be. As much as it aligns with the will and intention of God for your life, step into everything He has placed in front of you. This is not a license to make up stuff outside of His will and then try to get His approval. But if He said it and put it in you, do it, be it, become it.

It is only when we allow our full selves to be used and expressed that we can accurately depict and display the beauty of God.

Chapter 7

You'd Be Surprised
What a Little Belief Can Do

If you confess with your mouth that Jesus is Lord and believe in your heart that God raised him from the dead, you will be saved.
—Paul, Romans 10:9, ESV

I remember exactly where I was when I first saw the animated basketball film *Space Jam*, a movie that feels as much a part of my childhood as Fruity Pebbles and flag football. I cannot recall how many times I sat glued in front of my TV wearing my *Space Jam* matching jersey and shorts, watching Michael Jordan and Bugs Bunny take on the Monstars. I don't want to brag, but my parents somehow managed to get me the Jordan 11s from the film. I wore them almost every day. (That is, until I lost them in Orlando on a family vacation, an event that still haunts me to this day.)

That movie captured the imagination of every child of the nineties. If you weren't a Looney Tunes fan, you were a Michael Jordan fan. If you weren't a basketball fan, you at least knew who MJ was. If you didn't know who MJ was, you were probably living under a rock.

And if you didn't know Bugs, basketball, or Black Jesus (MJ), you knew the feature song on the *Space Jam* soundtrack, "I Believe I Can Fly":

I believe I can fly
I believe I can touch the sky[1]

We all knew it. And not only did we know the song but many of us tried to reenact the song.

DO YOU BELIEVE YOU CAN FLY?

If you were between the ages of three and thirteen (or maybe even thirty) when that movie came out, you definitely tied some cape-like fabric around your neck, climbed up on a couch, bed, or maybe even a rooftop, and jumped off while singing this song at the top of your lungs. For those few moments, you did it. You were soaring just like the birds in the sky, not a care in the world, free and flying just like you knew you could. As you began to adjust to your new atmosphere, however, there was a sudden shift. You soared until gravity said nope. The song had superpowers until it didn't. You came crashing back down to earth, realizing it was only a song and not your reality.

The impact of this song was profound not because of its musical structure or catchy lyrics but because it was anchored in a core human principle, a key factor in the human experience that propels us through hardship and into a future we can only dream of. What is it? *Belief.*

We All Dare to Believe

We all have something we dare to hope or believe in. Even if you are not a person of faith or don't have a clearly articulated code of morality you live by, you still have a set of beliefs. We all believe in something—even if your something is nothing (which is interesting to me, since it seems like a much further leap of faith to believe in nothing than something).

Belief. We all have it; we all do it. It has the power to take humans to places that no one thought possible. It fuels dreams and provides hope for a reality we cannot yet see. The song "I Believe I Can Fly" was a worldwide sensation because it resonated with something deep inside every soul: the desire to believe in something that seems almost impossible.

During my time on this spinning ball we call Earth, I have been connected with the effects and power of belief my entire life.

Let me share a little bit about that.

A Pastor's Kid from Bowling Green

I grew up a PK ("pastor's kid"). I spent most of my Sundays, Wednesdays, and occasionally all week within the four walls of a church. I listened to my dad preach his heart out every Sunday for a room of a little more than sixty people. Every week we would sing, pray, and speak about a God who offers hope, grace, healing, strength, and love. I grew up with my life built on belief. My childhood was spent observing my father and mother believe in the power of the local church. I watched as my aunt Lor-Lor and grandmother Nanaw believed for people to be healed and come to know Jesus. I was taught to believe in the power of prayer and miracles—that the God of the Bible is not just a fairy tale but is alive and active to this day, ready to move on behalf of His children. I grew up covered in the beauty, impact, and power of belief.

As I have gotten older, the power of belief has not left my heart. I still am certain of all those things I believed sitting in that front row in that small church building in Bowling Green. I believe God can do anything, that He is almighty and all-powerful. He is still the miracle-working, promise-keeping, body-raising, sickness-healing, relationship-repairing, soul-snatching savior He showed Himself to be two thousand years ago. I believe He is madly in love with every human on this planet and He has a plan for you reading this book right now.

That's what I believe.

Whether you believe what I believe or not, we can agree that belief has power. In fact, I've come to realize that, at times, belief can be more powerful than reality.

Belief Is Bigger Than Reality

Have you ever met someone who can sing but believed they cannot? You hear them quietly humming a perfectly pitched melody. You say, "Hey, you can sing!"

"Oh, no, I could never!" they reply.

You look at them with that Russell–Westbrook side-eye, thinking, *What? You trippin'!* The reality is, they *can* sing. There's only one problem: Somewhere, sometime, there was a break between their reality and their belief. Maybe when they were younger and not as confident, they tried to sing and someone made fun of them. Maybe they never received the encouragement they needed, or maybe they didn't like the attention of performing. Whatever the reason, somewhere along the way a belief was planted that choked out reality. They believe they cannot sing, so they don't.

On the other hand, perhaps you've met someone who believes they can sing when in fact they cannot. I am talking about those crazy-faith, singing-like-they-got-Grammys type of people. They walk around wailing at the top of their lungs like someone is paying them for every note they attempt. My friend Brie is like that. I think she can actually sing, or at least hold a note, but what you mainly hear from her is some deep *hallelujaaaaaaah* or some old rap song that she has transposed into a new key being belted out in grand vibrato like she's Adele or Whitney. Brie believes she can sing, so she sings.

The third type are the unicorns. They come once in a generation. They are the ones who believe they can sing and, in reality, *can* sing. They are gifted and confident. They have honed their gift like a mighty weapon and know exactly how to use it. They work with the unstoppable mixture of belief and reality. When these two things collide, watch out. This individual will turn the world upside down.

The One-Two Punch of Belief and Reality

There is tension between reality and belief. When it comes to these two things, there are only two outcomes: Your belief either *cripples* your reality or *cultivates* it.

The title of this book carries an underlying assumption: that there is a God. Before you can live in the power of the truth of being chosen, you must first decide whether you believe in His existence. While I could spend the next ten pages explaining why I hold this belief, ultimately, it is a decision you must make for yourself.

I am of the strong conviction that the most logical and rational foundation is the fact that there is an ultimate Designer behind all the beauty we see: God. Though you do not have to share this conviction, I have chosen to anchor my life in this belief. Among all the beautiful things God has created, humans are His most prized possession. He not only cares for us but has uniquely chosen each of us for a specific purpose. I would love to transport this conviction into the recesses of your soul and spirit, but that is a step you will have to take for yourself. With all your pain, problems, and pettiness (come on, some of us are petty), God has still chosen you. And the implications of this reality are not only immediate but eternal. The course of history and your future will be drastically changed if you believe three simple words: *God Chose Me.*

Before we dive into the implications of this reality, however, we must first address the matter of belief. I submit to you that the power of this reality is only as potent as your belief.

You see, we all have a choice before us. That choice is to believe God or spend our lives running from, arguing against, or ignoring that truth. *You are chosen.* But do you believe it? Do you really, wholeheartedly believe that the God of the universe has chosen you?

The belief I speak of is neither an empty optimism nor a fake faith but rather a genuine belief that is reinforced by conviction and confession. If you are anything like me, the journey to this authentic belief may take some time, some practice, and even some failure—but you can get there. I am living proof. Although I am authoring a book on the power of this belief, I have spent much of my life void of the confidence that comes from believing I am chosen by God. I cannot tell you how many nights I spent questioning my capability. How many opportunities I missed— not because I wasn't good enough but because I *believed* I wasn't.

For a long time, the reality of being chosen was crippled by my belief that I was too bad and too broken to be chosen by such an incredible God. I mean, why would He choose me? I am inconsistent. I lie. I change my mind. I am weak. I fail time and again. I've made mistake after mistake. Done the very thing I swore never to do. And then done it again. For years, these were the doubts that ran rampant in my mind, playing on the big screen of my soul, seemingly the only station my antenna could pick up. They felt endless in length and grew louder by the day.

And they still do sometimes.

I would be lying if I told you I don't have doubts. Please don't think that I always walk around screaming "God Chose Me!" and never question what He's called me to do. I wrestle with the effect of my beliefs on reality every day.

For example, I was horrible at English class. I mean *horrible*. I'll never forget the first paper I had to write for school. I turned each sentence into a rambling run-on, thinking I would sound smart or profound. I got a D on that paper. You think I haven't had flash-backs of that while writing this book? The reality is, I have never written a book before. But I have a choice. Do I believe that be-cause I have never done this, I could never do it? Or do I choose to believe that God knows what He put inside me and choose to work with Him to make this book a reality?

I was excited and terrified when we had our son, Arlo. In fact, I was so messed up I went into a three-week depression starting the day he was born. The pressure, the fear—*What if I screw him up?*—it was too much. The reality was, I had never had a kid before. And so, I had a choice: I could believe in the weakest parts of me, or I could choose to believe that God knew what He was doing when He made me Arlo's father—that I was going to be not only a good dad but the *perfect* dad for Arlo.

I could go on and on about the many times I've had to wrestle to believe, but here is the cold, hard truth: Belief is a decision.

Yes, you *decide* to believe.

BELIEF IS A DECISION

Perhaps you've been told that belief is something more than that. It's not some magical fairy dust like the kind Tinker Bell uses to help Peter Pan fly. I wish that was true. However, you either decide to believe or not. You can talk about evidence and facts and probability, but ultimately, you trust what you believe not because you have facts but because you decided to.

Take marriage, for example. There are no guarantees in marriage. You have no way of knowing what will happen, who you will become, or how they will treat you. Still, you decide to commit. To believe in the future with them.

There is also no guarantee your car won't blow up while you're driving down the road. Your car literally utilizes gas to produce little explosions. You choose to believe—dare I say *trust*—that whoever made the car knew what they were doing. You *decide*. You don't pray before you start your car. You don't wait for a sign from God. You don't read the owner's manual or learn how to build a combustion engine before you drive. You *decide* that the person who made the car is smarter than you, and you turn the ignition. You trust the maker of the car.

In my generation, there has been a mass exodus from traditional faith, ethics, and specifically Christian faith. There are numerous valid and reasonable factors contributing to this shift. With that being said, I want to directly address the reality that, at some point, you must confront the question of where your strength will come from. If we rip apart truth, faith, and God, all that will be left is us. And, friend, I love you, but we are neither that good nor strong! Humans have no business trying to govern or control life. We have proven that we are absolutely terrible at it! So, I submit that, for just a moment, you rejuvenate your belief.

At some point you will have to decide to believe. That is it. You'll have to decide to trust the Maker. You will have to decide that the life you want is on the other side of your belief. You could live your whole life worried, afraid, and questioning every car you get into. But it would be a very fearful life, and you would be late to everything. Or you could decide, "You know what, at this point, walking and breathing is a risk. Love is a risk. Life is a risk. So, I am going to choose to believe that today is in God's hands, He has a plan, He knows what He's doing, and most of all, He chose me."

THE MIRACLE OF BELIEF

The power of belief is most beautifully articulated in Paul's letter to the church in Rome. He was writing to a group of people who were being persecuted heavily at the time. Families were being split apart. Homes were being destroyed. People were even being killed for their belief in Jesus. In communicating to them how to enter into this miraculous salvation, Paul gave them two words: "If you *confess* with your mouth that Jesus is Lord and *believe* in your heart that God raised him from the dead, you will be saved" (Romans 10:9, ESV, emphasis mine). I believe Paul's letter is meant for us as it was for the church in Rome. People may take your home, your clothes, even your family, but they cannot take the belief you have in your heart. And that's worth more than anything.

Friend, the world is a crazy place. There seem to be more questions and fewer answers than ever. I cannot prove to you with empirical data that you are chosen. If that's what you are requiring, this is not the book for you. However, if you are courageous enough to decide to believe that you are chosen by God, you will be uniquely positioned to live a life of hope, joy, peace, confidence, and contentment. I cannot force it upon you, and I cannot make the decision for you. It is yours and yours alone.

Consider God's message to the people of Israel through Moses in Deuteronomy 30:19: "Today I have given you the choice between life and death, between blessings and curses. Now I call on heaven and earth to witness the choice you make. Oh, that you would choose life, so that you and your descendants might live!"

I pray you choose to believe that you are chosen by God, not just for you but for those who will come after you.

In this moment, I set before you a choice: belief or unbelief. Trust or distrust. Acceptance or rejection. The choice is yours. If I could, I would jump through these pages and push you into this new life. I sincerely pray that you would choose to believe, receive, and recite the reality that God chose you. I am not saying magic fairy dust will fall the moment you decide to believe. In fact, I don't know that we can ever complete the process of belief. It is a daily journey with daily commitment.

As I write these very words, I still must choose to believe that I am chosen. I am not claiming that this belief will change your situation—but it will change *you*. From anxious to at peace. Worried to willing. Tired to trusting. Comparing to confident. Constantly running to content. If that is an exchange you desire, let your new day begin. You can fly. You are chosen. Now is the time to believe it.

Chapter 8

BETTER WATCH YOUR WORDS

Words are free. It's how you use them that may cost you.
—Rev. J. Martin, The Power of Words

Abby Rose Henry. I remember the first time I saw her. I was an hour deep in an Instagram search for "cool people in Tulsa." I had just moved for my new job as a youth pastor and was trying to find friends in the city. I rolled across the hashtag #sociality. (If you remember that, you are an OG. If not, don't worry—you weren't missing anything.) This tiny, hippie blonde popped up on my page. She was equal parts beautiful and mysterious. I could feel the warmth of her spirit through my phone. I could tell she was kind and gracious, full of love and light. I immediately followed and began to creep her IG. I went all the way back to the beginning, searching for, let's be honest, a boyfriend. Fast-forward a couple of weeks, and I was standing in the lobby of church on Easter Sunday, and in she walked, the girl from Instagram. She was everything I had seen and more. She had a quiet curiosity about her. Not to mention that Instagram failed to capture her full beauty! I casually waved as she walked past, trying to keep it super cool—only to freak out once she was no longer looking my way.

Immediately after the service was over, I sent her a DM saying, "Hey, I just saw you, I think I love you, let's get married"—or something to that effect. Without giving you all the details of our story, in May 2016 we got married in Phoenix, Arizona. After leading a youth ministry, starting a church, and traveling Europe doing wedding photography, we eventually found ourselves volunteering at this tiny church on the north side of Tulsa called Transformation Church. I had met the pastor, Michael Todd, about six months earlier, and he'd been the lead pastor for about a year at that time. That season changed our lives forever.

Along my journey with Abby Rose, there have been many special moments. However, out of all the moments we have had together, none compares to the adventure of starting a family.

OUR (NOT SO) LITTLE FAMILY

In 2019 we brought home our firstborn, a son, Arlo Phoenix Metcalf. My goodness, he changed everything. I remember the first moment I held him—it was like no feeling I'd ever had. The love, protection, responsibility—it all flooded in like a tsunami. We would go on to have three girls, all sixteen months apart. Yep, we've had sex exactly four times and each time it worked! I'm joking. We have sex every chance we get. We literally have a sign in our bedroom that says Room Rules, and number 3 is "Have Good Sex."

Anyway.

It's crazy to think that we have four kids. From an Instagram search to an entire family! It feels so surreal.

I love being a father. In fact, I wanted to be a father before I wanted to be anything else. When I was eight years old, my little brother, and best friend, came into this world. Simply having a little brother made me love the idea of one day being a dad. It's all I've ever wanted, and I love every second. I love being Arlo, Luna, Jade, and Blue's father. They keep me humble, in prayer, and laughing. There is nothing like a conversation with an extravagantly articulate five-year-old or trying to have a calm discussion with a passionate little girl who's trying to find her makeup she bought two seconds ago. Or the joys of trying to break up World War III at bath time. It can be a little crazy at times, but Abby and I wouldn't change it for the world. They are the joy of our life, and we couldn't be more grateful to be Mom and Dad.

WHO WILL WE BE?

When our children were born, we both felt immense responsibility. We knew that each one of our kids was uniquely different and would require detailed love and attention. One responsibility I felt immediately was that of affirming their identity and security. As I am sure we all have experienced, most of us spend the early parts of our childhood and adolescence trying to discover who we are. We do this by exploring hobbies, interests, friend groups, music, culture, our family, and a plethora of other outlets. All in an attempt to grasp for some sense of belonging, recognition, and affirmation.

As a father I am keenly aware that this is a natural process all my children will go through. That being said, as I thought about their journey in life, I knew I wanted to be a solid foundation for my kids. There are some things I did not want them to have to search for or discover but that I wanted to impart to them—almost like a starting identity, a starting color palette, that they could build from and expand on. I didn't want to convey this in a demanding or controlling way but in the way a father desires the best for his children. I wanted to decide something that would help alleviate years of searching.

To accomplish this, my wife and I created some daily confessions for our children. I got the original idea from Mike (the pastor I met who has now become my best friend, boss, brother, and book agent). Any time we were on a trip together, I would overhear him on FaceTime with his girls: "You're the head and not the . . ."

"Tail!"

"Above and never . . ."

"Beneath!"

It was the cutest thing to hear those girls screaming affirmations over the phone. From that, Abby and I took some time to write out affirmations that we could say daily with our children, not only to establish but to affirm who they are and what it means to be a Metcalf. After some time, convos, and edits, this is what we came up with:

Metcalfs carry . . .
Peace and Purpose
Kindness and Compassion
Boldness and Bravery
Love and Light
In Jesus's name,
Amen

(We later added "Because God Chose Me.")

Every day, without fail, Arlo blurts out, "DADDDDD, don't forget our confessions." He loves leading his sisters and any excuse to tell them what to do. Over the past four years, it has been so fun to see these affirmations play out in daily life. For example, when Arlo is feeling nervous about going to school or trying something new, I will say, "Hey, bud, what do Metcalfs carry?"

"Boldness and Bravery."

"And what does that mean, son?"

"We can do hard things," he says in the cutest five-year-old way.

"All right, you got this!" And then he does something he was not previously prepared to do. Why? The situation was not eliminated; he did not suddenly forget how he was feeling. Nothing changed except one thing: his confession.

You See What You Say

As I've said, at the core of belief is a decision. However, I have discovered that in the process of making our decisions, we often need to water our choice with the power of confession.

When your confession changes, so do your beliefs—and when your belief changes, so do your actions.

The secret to sustaining a belief is consistent confession.

And therein lies the key to the belief that God chose you: If you find yourself struggling to believe it, start confessing it. And watch what happens.

Typically, we think of confession as an acceptance or admission of guilt. For example, if your mom asks you, "Did you eat all the Oreos?" you have an opportunity to lie or confess the truth. At its core, confession is accepting the reality of something that is happening or has happened. It is a verbal confirmation that agrees with a reality that is rooted either in fact or in lies. What does that mean?

Your confession does not have to be accurate to have authority.

The Consequence of Confession

Have you ever seen that crazy Netflix docuseries where the police get people to confess to things they didn't do? It's tragic to see the effect fear and manipulation can have on an individual or a group of individuals. Based on the promise of freedom or safety, a non-guilty party will sometimes confess to something they know they did not do just to get out from under the pressure of the current situation. But after feeling some initial relief, they begin to realize the horrible mistake they made. Why? Because now that they have confessed, there will be consequences they cannot reverse. They will have to pay the price for the confession they gave. True or not, their confession has consequences.

The same is true of you. Your confessions will always have consequences. Let me say it clearly:

The life you are living is the direct result of your confessions.

For example, let's say you are about to take a test and right before the test you start to second-guess your preparation. You fear that maybe you didn't review the right content. You question your ability to retain information, and all you can think is, *You always do this. You can never remember the right thing.* You start rehearsing failure in your mind. It goes from a moment of insecurity to an internal confession. You stop thinking about the hours you have put in and start thinking, *I don't know the right information. I am not good under pressure.* Over and over. By the time you get to the test, you have completely deflated your confidence. You feel as though there is no point in even taking the test. You just know you are going to fail, regardless of the effort, energy, hours of study, even the other test that you did well on. That insecurity has grown into a repeated confession that shakes your belief in yourself.

Maybe your confessions have affected your relationships.

Against your instincts you take the risk of putting yourself out there to someone you are interested in. As it turns out, they reciprocate the feelings you shared. You begin to date, and it's going better than expected. You begin to picture yourself with this person long-term. It really looks like y'all are the perfect match. But then worry and insecurity begin to creep in. You start to remember that you have thought things were good before and then out of nowhere the rug was swept out from under you. So, what do you do? To protect yourself you start to internally confess, "We are okay, but I am fine if it doesn't work." Slowly your internal dialogue goes from the joy of the relationship to the silent countdown until it falls apart. "This always happens to me. I'm just not built for relationships." Your confessions have reinforced a belief, and that belief has influenced your actions.

Or perhaps you're an athlete. You are consistent in training, disciplined in your diet, and intentional in your preparation. However, when it comes to the biggest moments, you cannot get that one failure out of your mind. Your confession goes from "You are prepared" to "Don't blow it." Now that's all you see: when you screwed up the big moment.

Maybe you are not an elite athlete but an elite parent. Instead of having confidence that God selected you to be the parent for your child, you begin to confess, "I've already messed up too much." So, instead of being there when your child needs you, you shy away out of guilt and shame.

In all these examples we can see that confession has the power to misguide our lives. Many of us can acknowledge the importance of positive confession for an impressionable child or an elite athlete. But when it comes to our own lives—to how we talk to ourselves about our relationships, finances, risks, faith, prayer, dreams, or future—it can't be that big of a deal, right?

My friend, there is no limit to the value of your confession. Whether you are a child developing confidence, an Olympian about to compete in the biggest event of your life, or a mom of two, your confessions have authority over not only your present but also your future. Our confessions are not just positive language or Pinterest wallpapers that make us feel better. The words God has given us to speak over ourselves and our families have the power to create worlds! Oh, you didn't know? Your words create worlds.

YOUR WORDS CREATE WORLDS

In Genesis 1, we get a picture of an earth without the creativity and order of God. It is a complete mess. An abyss with no order and no hope; a sea and sky of nothingness. Completely void of light and life. Now, depending on your theological and religious convictions, we may vary in our beliefs on how things began. Many postmodern thinkers have agreed on the Big Bang theory. Millions of years ago there was a slight vibration right before the explosion many scientists believe began the earth. I have no interest in debating this reality, nor is this an endorsement for the Big Bang; however, unlike popular Christian culture, I believe there is an intersection between the Bible and the belief many mainstream scientists hold. It is stated that milliseconds before this Big Bang, a small vibration ripped its way through the universe. This raises the question: What happened right before the Big Bang happened? What could it be? It is my belief that Genesis 1:3 gives us the answer:

God said, "Let there be light."

Boom!

Seconds before everything existed, there was one thing that

came: words. Not just any words, but God's word. *The* Word. The world came to be through the power of words. I bring this up because Scripture is clear that you and I are made in the image of God. So, if God's words have the power to create the world, what power lies within your vocal cords?

The Bible says, "Life and death are in the power of the tongue" (Proverbs 18:21, HCSB). I've heard that scripture my whole life. But could it be true? Is it possible that the life you are living is a result of the words you say? I am not speaking of the New Age idea of manifesting but of the God-given authority and power He has placed within each individual on this planet. Your words create worlds. But do you like the world you have created?

If your answer is yes, then *perfect*. You are a superstar and probably have a close relationship with Jesus. If you are more like me and there is even the slightest portion of your life that you believe could be improved, then this next section is for you.

You are not hopeless. You are not subject to your situation. You are not powerless in this moment, but instead you are empowered to see something new start now.

Although I am not sure who originally said it, my favorite quote is, "The best time to plant a tree was twenty years ago. The second best time is today." If you find yourself in a situation, mindset, cycle, relationship, addiction, or thought pattern you are not happy with, you have the opportunity to create a new pattern.

Studies in neuroscience have shown how positive and negative thoughts can shape the brain through neuroplasticity, the brain's ability to reorganize itself by forming new neural connections.[1] Positive words and thoughts are linked to the release of feel-good chemicals like dopamine and serotonin, promoting the formation of pathways that support optimism and emotional resilience. Conversely, negative words can activate stress responses, strengthening neural pathways associated with fear and anxiety.[2]

Your words matter. I've said it, science says it, God says it—will you believe it? They have the power to transform how you see the world, yourself, and your situation. It is time to take control of the words you say. If you are struggling to accept the reality and implications that God chose you, you are not alone. We all have struggled with accepting and receiving love. I write this book not from a place of arrival but from being on the journey myself.

In fact, in the last year I have had to completely exchange my most prominent and powerful internal confession. It all stems from a missed free throw.

THE FREE THROW

I grew up playing basketball and being absolutely obsessed with Allen Iverson. I never had cornrows, but I had all the jerseys, the do-rag, the velour tracksuit, and even the silver Jesus piece to set off the fit. Iverson was an icon. He still is. I heard one reporter say, "Michael Jordan made basketball popular, and Iverson made basketball cool." Allen Iverson seemed to live with the "God Chose Me" attitude before this book was even a thought. And following him, I tried to do the same thing.

There was one night I'll never forget. It was before one of our big games. I snuck into my dad's bedroom and stole a dress sock from his drawer. I went downstairs, grabbed scissors from the kitchen, and cut off the end. What was I doing? The year was 2006, and at this time they didn't make basketball shooting sleeves for skinny little kids like me. So I made my own. Yep, that's right. I wore a Dillard's dress sock on my left arm so I could be like Allen Iverson.

We were playing our biggest rival, Goodpasture. The game was intense, as it always was. I had had a great game and was facing off against my archnemesis, Chase. (Chase, if you're reading this, no hard feelings.) We were both point guards for our teams, and we played each other during middle school.

The game was in its final moments and we were down by one. Coach called a time-out, and we drew up a play. The ball would come to me. If I made the shot, I would go down in history as the coolest and best player to ever play. At least that's how I felt. I got the ball and drove to the lane, went up, and missed—but I was fouled. Them boys couldn't guard me. Two shots.

I started crying. I was not doing well under pressure, and I had no good confessions yet to help. I shot the first one and it hit the back of the rim and bounced out. I tried to calm myself down, to do my shooting routine. I could still tie the game. The second shot went up . . .

It rattled around the rim for what seemed like an eternity, hopped on the right side of the rim a couple of times, and then tipped over the side. I missed.

We lost. Because of me.

In that moment I felt shame, embarrassment, and so many other emotions. But the biggest emotion I felt was the sense of being a fraud. In my head I was good enough to be the captain of the team. Good enough to have the ball at the last second. However, I was not good enough to make the shot. I was close but not close enough. Good but not good enough. I wish I could say that sixth-grade moment was just a blip on my emotional radar, but somehow it stuck with me. This moment somehow fastened itself to me and began to wear away at my confidence and security. It gradually changed my internal dialogue from one of expectation and confidence to negativity and insecurity.

Years later and I'm sitting on my friend Carl's couch telling that same story, and he asks me, "What effect did that event have on your mind?" I muddle through different emotions and thoughts but eventually say, "Most of the time I am thinking I can't do it and I'm probably not as good as I think I am."

"Really?" he says in that loving yet sarcastic way of his. "And where has that confession got you?" I sit there and begin to cry as I grapple with the reality of how deep this insecurity has taken root.

For fifteen years, that was the confession that played in my head on repeat. Leading, preaching, parenting, being a husband, walking down the street, no matter what I was doing, this message—that I am not as good as I think—kept popping into my head. What I heard was, "I can't do this and I'm not good enough." Without realizing it, one moment of failure had shaped my confession for years.

After I dried my tears, Carl helped me construct a new confession. I wrote it down. I even turned it into a screen saver on my phone. It says:

I am completely capable of anything I put my mind to and I am way better than I think at everything I do.

Now, you may hear that and think, *Charles, that's a little dramatic.* For you, maybe. But perhaps you haven't spent fifteen years telling yourself that you're not capable. My old confession had over twenty years to create pathways in my mind. To change those pathways, I had to write something so clear and confident that it would shake me out of those old self-defeating ways. One day I may not need it. But for now, if you look at my phone you will see a confession that I am working on believing every day. Why? Because what I confess has authority over my reality. When I read that confession, it reminds me that I walk with a God-given untouchable confidence. It reminds me not to live small and safe but to live the unstoppable Holy Spirit–inspired life that is willing to fall, willing to take risks, and willing to make a move!

A Better Confession

Here I want to offer a list of example confessions. They were not written with your personal story in mind. That is something we can do together in the study guide that goes along with this book. But these can be a beautiful starting place for you to rewire your brain to believe the best about you and your future. As you take hold of your thoughts, you will begin to experience a transformation that goes beyond speech and seeps into the deepest parts of your soul and spirit.

I have what it takes for today.

I am capable.

I can grow and change

I am loved and even liked.

I am a joy to be around.

I am not what happened to me.

I am not the sum of my failures.

I can learn from my mistakes and failures.

I can do hard things.

I am treasured.

I am needed by friends.

I can show up for someone today.

I can show up for myself today.

I carry the peace and presence of God with me.

God has given me what I need.

By God's grace, today can be a better day.

As you begin to write your own confessions, please remember that this is not empty positivity or self-reliance. This is proclaiming the truth that God, your creator, has already spoken over you. These statements are written with the understanding that you cannot do anything by yourself. That without Christ you do not have the strength, peace, and purpose that you need. You are only as good as God allows. You do not have all the answers, but empowered by His Spirit, you can do all things!

The very power that spoke the Milky Way into existence. The same words that formed the fish of the sea. That same power resides in you. Your words matter, and they have the potential to build a life that you have only dreamed of. This is not "name it and claim it" or manifestation. This is the very DNA of God that makes His home within you. It is time to take control of your words. As moms everywhere over the last century have said: "Watch your mouth."

THE MIC IS LIVE

I have spent the past eleven years speaking into a microphone. One of the first lessons I learned was that once you hold the mic, you must conduct your speech in a way that assumes the mic is on. You never want to be the person who gets played by the sound guy and says something that was private but gets blasted over the speakers for everyone to hear. No, you want to live like the mic is on. I'll never forget being in an auditorium and suddenly hearing a door close, a zipper, and then what sounded like Niagara Falls. Yep, one of my friends had accidentally left his mic on while using the bathroom. The mic was on.

My point? Your mic is on. God is listening. He cares what you have to say, and your words carry weight. If you don't want to see it, don't say it. And if you believe it, you better speak it.

Your new mind and new world are shaped by your words. What will you say? How will you use the power that has been placed in your hands? Your words matter—they can either build a prison or a platform, a cage or a castle. My suggestion? Use your words to build a world where you and those you love can live in for a long time!

A Book Break for
Slow Readers Like Me

In the previous chapters, we have laid the foundation for an untouchable confidence by rooting ourselves in the reality that God chose us. My hope is that you have been able to see some key values that will begin to anchor themselves in your soul. In fact, when preparing to write this book, I first saw it as an image or diagram before any other ideas formed.

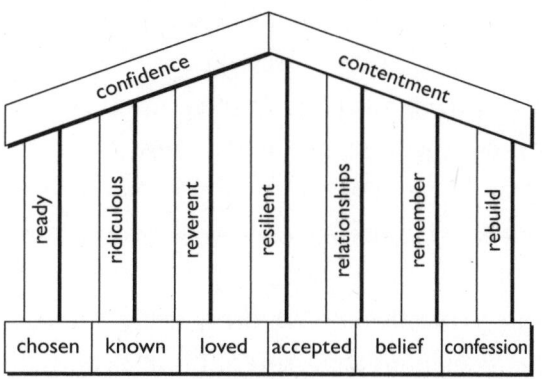

confidence   contentment

ready | ridiculous | reverent | resilient | relationships | remember | rebuild

chosen | known | loved | accepted | belief | confession

As you can see in this diagram, this book is built on six anchors that are essential if we are going to live with an untouchable confidence: Chosen, Known, Loved, Accepted, Belief, and Confession. These values are the building blocks for an unstoppable life. They serve as the foundation for each of the chapters that we have worked through—the key ingredients to the five-star meal we are hoping to put together and present to the world. It is by understanding, embracing, and reminding yourself of these values that you will be able to be who God has called you to be.

After you have grasped the six anchors, you will build the following seven attitudes: Ready, Ridiculous, Reverent, Resilient, Remember, Relationships, and Rebuild. The following chapters are more of a resource or index. They are not written as sequential ideas or building-block concepts but are meant to be read and comprehended as standalone ideas. I hope that as you read through the next chapters you will find yourself relating to and identifying with different ideas. If you dive into a concept and feel like it does not speak to you, no worries. Although I painstakingly wrote each chapter and believe them to be beneficial, I do want to put you in the driver's seat. I am simply here as your guide as we journey together.

As you read, I want you to be inquisitive and reflective. Each chapter is meant to inspire you toward an attitude and action. Let me take a moment to clarify what I mean.

I believe that life is all about attitude. Another way I could articulate attitude is posture. When I say "posture," I am not speaking about standing straight up with your shoulders back. I am talking about your *internal* posture—your attitude, demeanor, and disposition.

For example, consider my daughter Jade. When we are together, she is always in an internal posture to find the funny. In any situation, she is looking for humor and joy. My brother Chandler is the same way. Whether Jade is in dance class or getting disciplined for sneaking a cookie, her heart is always leaning in to find joy and laughter. Though the situation may not seem appropriate to find humor in, her internal posture looks for what she has decided is important. And she always finds what she's looking for.

These next few chapters operate similarly. We will explore seven postures that will give you a lens to look through, an attitude to guide your life. I pray you have a ready spirit that is looking for what God might be doing or saying through any moment.

Take a moment to look over the diagram again. At the top of this structure rests confidence and contentment. These two ideas have served as both the seeds and goal of this book. Even before I wrote the first word of this book, these two ideas were deep in my spirit. The most powerful contentment and confidence come from those who truly believe they are chosen by God and see the world through that filter. In other words, knowing they ultimately belong to God shapes their decisions and directs their thoughts. So, here is the key question you need to address: How would you live if you believed you were chosen by God?

For those of you having trouble answering this, let me help. First, imagine yourself with untouchable confidence. For some, this may seem completely out of reach; for others, it may not be a big jump. But go with me. Complete confidence. Not in superficial, external things. Sure, I want you to be confident in your appearance, but I am speaking of something deeper—a confidence in who you are at the core. A trust in yourself. A trust that you have great ideas. That you show up believing you have something of value to offer. That you interact in every relationship with trust that you are enough. That you try, knowing that if you fail it is not the end but just the beginning. In fact, you don't worry about failing because failure is simply a step on the path to improvement. No second-guessing, no backing up, no shying away. You are willing to try and try again. Willing to speak up, stand out, stand up, and never sacrifice who you are. Imagine you are completely confident.

Now add to that unshakable confidence a deep contentment. My friend, now you are dangerous. Not only are you confident to try anything but you are content with nothing. You are confident to start something but content if it does not work. You are confident to speak up but content if the idea doesn't get used. You are confident to put yourself out there but are okay if others say no, because you value you. You are confident enough to trust that you hear God but content enough if it takes a while before you see Him move. Confident enough to pray with faith that God can answer but content enough to know that even if He doesn't, one day you will be home with Him. Confident enough to swing for the fences but content enough to watch someone else win the game. This, my friend, is an almost nonexistent way of living. You are a force to be reckoned with because you are confident and content.

I don't want this to be just a thought experiment or brief moment of reflection. This can be your life. In fact, I believe this life awaits you. This is how you were made to live and who you were created to be. You have everything you need to be confident and content. You have the makeup to carry yourself with a deep sense of love, appreciation, and value for who you are. This is not a hope or wish. This is the life that stands on the other side of your agreement with the truth that God chose you.

Are you ready to step into this new life? Are you ready to stop living in the shadow of your own insecurities? Are you ready to give up the frustration of being stuck in the same cycle? Are you ready to let go of your tendency to compare yourself with others?

Are you ready to start sharing your ideas with others? I was. That is why I wrote this book.

As we move forward, I want you to think about how you could implement these attitudes or postures into your daily life. How could you transform them from words on a page into fuel that powers your life? It will take time and intentionality, but I believe that if you embrace these ideas wholeheartedly you will see a miraculous shift, not only in how you feel but in the life you live. Are you ready?

Let's begin.

Chapter 9

READY WHEN YOU ARE

If you're always ready, you ain't gotta get ready.
—Granny Estelle

My wife, Abby Rose, and I have been together for ten years now. It has been the most beautiful and enjoyable journey to grow together. I was twenty-two and she was twenty when we married. In the first months of our engagement, people would look shocked when we told them we were getting married. They would then adopt a patronizing tone and begin explaining how hard marriage would be because we were so young. From the beginning, we decided to reject anyone else's story about our marriage. We were not marrying the people who had a negative opinion about when we should or shouldn't be getting married. We were making a commitment to and covenant with each other, and we were the only ones who would decide how our marriage was going to go. If it was going to be hard, it would be hard because we decided to make it that way. And if it was going to be fruitful, joyful, and full of love, it would be that way because we decided.

I wish I could tell you that this strong-willed decision eliminated all the trials of marriage. But just like any other married couple, we have had our fair share of challenges and are aware that we have many more ahead. Among those challenges, there is one specific story that stands out from early in our marriage. It was not a big deal, but it often comes to mind, and I'll feel the same frustration as I did at that moment.

ARE YOU READY YET?

Abby and I both enjoy clothes. In different ways, we both want to look nice, catch a vibe, swag out—whatever you want to call it. Although we share this same passion, we have completely different ways in how we go about it. Since about the sixth grade, I have picked out my clothes the night before. It can be a short process, or I can spend three hours meandering through my closet. Either way, it doesn't matter. Why? Because I have nowhere to be except in my bed. Abby, on the other hand, does not utilize this incredible tool of preparation, despite my many lectures on how it would benefit her life. She likes to wait until we are absolutely pressed for time, and only then does she start going through her clothes in a panic, looking for something to wear. Inevitably I end up sitting in the closet with her, trying to give her the green light that her outfit looks *great!* Now that you have this context, I present Exhibit A.

Abby and I had been married for about two months, and already this exact scenario had played out. I had not yet learned the art of helping her, so she was left to fend for herself in our tiny apartment closet. I was sitting on the couch looking at my phone while my favorite show, *The Office,* played in the background. After what felt like an eternity, Abby Rose walked out of our bedroom, looked at me, and said some of the wildest words she has ever uttered: "Ready when you are!"

What?

I replied with disgust and a little bit of drama: "Ready when I am? No way! I have been ready! You weren't ready when I was. I have been ready when you were, and you have not been ready!" She paused, looking at me in a confused manner. She could tell I was completely overreacting; however, I was also very passionate.

"Um . . . okay? I was just saying when you are ready, I am ready now."

"No . . . nope! Can't say that because now you're making it seem like you are waiting on me—and that is not the case! I picked out my clothes *last night* so this exact thing would not happen!"

"Okay, well, are you ready?"

"Yes, yes I am!"

Now, there are a couple of observations from this story that I would like to draw out. One, Abby should be picking out her clothes the night before (can I get an amen?). Also, I may or may not be overly dramatic. And lastly, if God said to you, "Ready when you are," what would be your response?

ARE YOU READY IF GOD CALLS?

Many of us have believed what I think could be one of the most misleading misconceptions, and that is: "You are waiting on God." The Scriptures are very clear on how different God's timeline is from ours. In Isaiah, God declares that His ways are "higher" than our ways and that His thoughts are *absolutely* nothing like ours (Isaiah 55:8–9).

Isaiah used a dramatic illustration to communicate how much God is *not* like us. He said, "As high as the heavens are above the earth" (GNT). Here is a fun fact about me: I can sometimes nerd out on very random information. For the sake of a leadership talk I once gave, I actually researched how high the heavens are above the earth.

How Big Is Space?

The original word for "heavens" in the Hebrew is *šāmayim*, pronounced "shaw-mah'-yim."[1] Among its definitions, one of the most common is "the known universe." Guess how big the known universe is? Ninety-three billion light-years in diameter.[2] Now, you may or may not know what a light-year is, unless, of course, you are Neil deGrasse Tyson or Buzz Lightyear. A light-year is the distance light can travel in one Earth year, which is 9.46 trillion kilometers, or 5.88 trillion miles.[3] According to modern research, Earth is about 46.5 billion light-years away from the edge of the universe. So let me do some Google math for you and make my point.

If Isaiah was on Joe Rogan with Neil deGrasse Tyson and was to give you an equation to figure out how much God thought like you, this would be it:

46.5 billion light-years × 5.8 trillion miles =

Now, I did some very rough calculations, and that means God's timeline and our timeline are roughly 27 quintillion miles apart.

Yes, 27 quintillion. That is 27 with nineteen zeros after it!

God Is Not Like Us

Now, why did I do this math? You need to know that God does not operate the way we operate. He doesn't think how we think. And you need to know that the suggestion that our small, finite minds have somehow managed to be so prepared that we have accomplished everything God has asked of us and can now sit on the couch of our life "waiting on Him"—well, my friend, that is *insane*. We are not waiting on God; God is waiting on us. Are you ready?

Perhaps you're thinking, *Okay, Charles, I am chosen. I get it—but chosen for what?* This is a beautiful journey that only you can embark on. It is filled with self-discovery, growth, wins, and losses, but it is this journey that sparks a flame in the human soul. If you're going to have the courage to begin the journey of a lifetime, you must be ready. Ready for what? Well, that part is up to God. It is simply our responsibility to posture ourselves to be ready for whatever, whenever.

Many of us have dreams, goals, and visions for our lives. Places we see ourselves going and things we want to do. The only catch is, if we were honest with ourselves, we do not currently possess the essential tools to arrive at or sustain the life we so desperately dream of. We must shift our perspective so that every day of our lives we wake up and live with a spirit that sees each day as an opportunity to prepare. An opportunity to get ready. We are living our only promised day and therefore should watch expectantly for what God might say or do.

WHO CALLED YOU?

If I called you and said I was forming an elite basketball team and needed your help, allowing you six months to prepare and promising a signing bonus if you performed well in tryouts, you would probably shrug, laugh, or even ignore my request. Why? Because the source from which this offer comes does not warrant much preparation. However, if you received a call from LeBron James presenting the same opportunity, there may be a slightly stronger and more enthusiastic response. Why? Because you realize who picked you determines how you prepare. This is infinitely truer when it comes to God. If He has chosen you for something, if He has set you apart for a unique calling, you have something great to get ready for. And the person calling you has the authority to position you where you need to be and the power to help you live out your calling.

BUILD IT WHEN YOU DON'T SEE IT

The story of Noah, found in Genesis, is a powerful account of faith, obedience, and someone with a ready posture. God instructed Noah to build a massive ark because He was going to send a great flood to destroy the wickedness on the earth. Scripture suggests that Noah had never seen a flood, so the concept of a global deluge would be beyond imagination (see Hebrews 11:7). Yet, despite the unbelief and the mocking from those around him, Noah trusted God's word and began preparing for what he couldn't see. He spent years building the ark according to God's precise instructions. Can you imagine? At some point Noah had to make the decision to believe God, but then his decision had to turn into preparation.

What are you preparing for that God has said but you cannot see?

What if, instead of sitting around waiting and wasting away, you decided to wake up with a fresh expectation? What if you began each day with a purpose in your spirit and joy in your heart, saying, "Today could be the day everything changes. Today could be the day God comes through. Today could be the day I form a relationship that changes my life." When you decide to live with this expectation, it shifts your life from passivity to preparation. You start seeing and living in the reality you are hoping for rather than where you feel stuck.

Maybe you see yourself running a nonprofit that serves the underprivileged. Instead of focusing on the fact that you don't have the funding, you begin writing a vision for when you have multiple sites and teams to serve people across your city.

Maybe you want to be a missionary to a foreign land. Instead of focusing on the fact that you've never been outside of your hometown, why not start studying world religions so you can be prepared to relate to and communicate with anyone?

Perhaps you see yourself having children. Instead of being unhappy because you're single, why don't you start reading books on leaving a legacy?

Maybe you want to be a philanthropist one day, but right now you can't see a way out of the tough spot you're in. Why not start giving away one dollar a week? If you think a dollar a week is too small an amount, think again. Why would you give away a million dollars when you don't give away one?

We do this so often. *I* do this so often. I ask God for something I am not prepared for at all. So instead of asking for something you may or may not have control over, why not use what is right in front of you to prepare for what God might do? Why not live in a position that says, "God, I am ready for what You want to do"? When you realize that God has chosen you and that He is preparing something for you, your only response should be a ready spirit.

I Want a Ready Spirit

My point is, I would hate to be sitting on the couch, waiting on God, when He offers me the opportunity I have dreamed of, believed for, and prayed for my entire life. I want to be ready. I want to be prepared.

And so I will live every day preparing and expecting for God to do something miraculous in my life! May the posture of my heart and your heart always be . . .

"God, I am ready when You are."

Once you realize you are chosen, the next question is, Are you ready? What if you did something once a week or once a month to prepare for where God is taking you. It doesn't have to be spectacular. What if it was just natural? In fact, what if it was *really natural*? Or even *super natural*.

What if God took your preparation for marriage, for college, for kids, for growth, for finances, for love, for ministry and used that as the measuring bar for what to give you? Would you like what you receive?

All I know is, when it comes time for God to talk to me, I want to be able to say, "Ready when You are!"

Chapter 10

I'M NOT AFRAID TO LIVE

The bitterest tears shed over graves are for words left unsaid and deeds left undone.
— *Harriet Beecher Stowe,* Little Foxes

For the past ten years, I have served as a pastor. This was not always the plan, nor was it a specific goal I set out for. However, Scripture says, "Many are the plans in a person's heart, but it is the LORD's purpose that prevails" (Proverbs 19:21, NIV). While it can be very frustrating when our plans don't come to fruition, I can confirm that God's plans are always better. With or without my participation and agreement, God has always guided me to what is best. Pastoring is exactly that for me. It has challenged me and matured me deeply.

As a pastor, I am often on a stage of some sort, with a microphone, encouraging people in some way. However, this is a substantially small part of pastoring. Nevertheless, it is part of what I do on a weekly basis. With this being the case, I have said many things and told many stories over the past ten years. Some I can recall, and others I would be shocked if you repeated them back to me. My tendency is, once the train has left the station, it's hard to bring it back.

Perhaps you've experienced that. Has there ever been a moment where you found yourself talking and simultaneously thinking, *What am I saying?* For me, one of these moments took place during one of our prayer services.

WHAT IN THE WORLD DID I JUST SAY?

If you've never been to a prayer service at Transformation Church, you're missing out. It is a mixture of spiritual fire, loud prayers, and some old-school church that is hard to find nowadays. If you come to a prayer service at TC, you are a *real one.* You're not there for the fluff or the "hype music"—you are there to encounter God and throw out some ro-to-ba-sha's!

One of these nights last year, I found myself leading prayer, and toward the end I felt pressed to encourage the room to live with boldness. I began speaking on why our God is the greatest. I do not recall exactly how I said it, but I somehow acknowledged the fact that God has taken the fear out of dying and out of living. Because of salvation and the promise of heaven, I do not have to fear death. And because of God's presence and power in my everyday life, I do not have to fear living each day. I wish it had come out that simple; however, what I proceeded to yell from the stage was, "I ain't afraid to live and I sure ain't afraid to die!"

Now, did it get the people going? Of course! Is it a wild thing to yell? Yes. But I really felt that way and still do. I remember coming off stage and thinking, *Yeah! That's true—I'm not afraid to live! God is with me, I am protected, and He has a plan!* Looking back, it was a spiritual sense of "untouchability" because I was so confident that God was with me and so much stronger than anything I would face. Beautiful, right? In about twelve hours, I would discover how much I believed it.

I Got Hit by a Car

The next morning, I woke up at five o'clock, just as I have done five days a week for the past two years. I went on my Tuesday-morning cycling ride with my friends. I have done this ride a million times and today was no different. We completed our normal twenty-five-mile route, and I was about two minutes away from home. I was riding down the same road I always do. I looked left, signaled for my turn, looked again, signaled again, and then I began to turn left. Just when I leaned into my left turn, I saw a large, fast-moving black object crashing into my hip. It was a car. It happened so fast and yet somehow also seemed to happen in slow motion. I remember looking down as the vehicle crashed into the left side of my body, thinking, *This is not happening*. The gentleman driving had misread my turn signal and tried to pass. I was hurled off my bike and into the road. I hit the ground and rolled to the sidewalk. Out of sheer panic, I attempted to jump to my feet to ensure I did not get hit again. As I tried to stand up, my legs gave out and I fell to the ground. While trying to maintain consciousness, the man who hit me walked up and tried to assist. He was completely shaken up as it was a genuine accident.

As we were trying to sort out whether to call an ambulance, my friend Moe happened to be passing by. He had taken a different route than normal to avoid traffic and saw me on the side of the road. He and the gentleman tried to help me to my feet, but I lost consciousness. From there, things get pretty fuzzy.

I made it to the hospital, where my wife and friends joined me. The doctors performed all sorts of scans, checked certain levels, and so on. They informed me that I had somehow escaped with no major injuries. I had a pretty severe concussion and some bad road rash along my elbow and butt. However, no fractured or broken bones and no internal bleeding. It was a full-blown miracle. God had protected me from what very well could have been a fatal crash.

As my wife and friends wheeled me to the car, I couldn't help but recall myself screaming, "I ain't afraid to live and I sure ain't afraid to die!" I laughed to myself and thought, *God, this isn't exactly what I meant.*

Since my accident, there has been an assortment of pressures, pains, and challenges to navigate. The crash could not have come at a worse time. As I write this book, I am still battling the mental challenges of a concussion. Some days I wake up forgetting what day it is and struggle to remember what I am doing while still trying to manage my daily responsibilities. It has shaken my confidence to the core and forced me to wrestle with the truth of what it really means to be chosen. However, with all the questions, conversations, counseling, and recovery, there has been one question I have had to ask myself: *Will fear steal my future?*

Is Fear My Only Future?

In addition to the physical pain from my bike crash, there has been far more non-physical damage. First, the fear of riding again. Something that had been an anchor for my mental and physical health now carried a level of fear and anxiety. There is also the anxiety it caused my wife. It was extremely hard to recover from receiving a call at 7 A.M. that your husband has been hit by a car and found unconscious on the side of the road. These are real moments and real fears that produced a real question, which we will focus on in this chapter: *How will you choose to live your life from this moment forward, in the midst of all the risk and fear that comes from falling?*

I don't know all that you have experienced in life. But no matter who you are or what you have walked through, I am 100 percent confident that you have experienced real moments of fear, pain, and hurt.

Maybe it was the pain of a failed relationship.

The failure of a business.

The shame of your past.

Maybe you have a physical injury you have never fully recovered from.

Maybe the pressure and pain of life have become too much to bear, and now you are stuck with an addiction you can see no way out of.

Maybe you have struggled with crippling anxiety.

Maybe you have felt so hopeless that you have contemplated taking your own life.

Fear in Your Bones

Any time the human body experiences trauma, there are myriad responses. These are hardwired into your programming, and they take over regardless of your personality type or background. Once you have experienced something that your body, mind, or spirit deems unsafe, your body immediately sends fear. This is actually a defense mechanism. Fear tells your body, "This is not safe and you need to be safe." It is a means of protection for your soul. The problem is, your body isn't great at determining when to stop feeling this fear. Even after you have left the traumatic situation, your body still thinks, *You need to be safe.* But life isn't safe.

Every human desires and deserves safety—physical, mental, and relational. These are innate, God-given needs. However, right next to your desire to be safe is the reality and risk of life. No matter how careful you are, no matter how cautious you may be, life is full of risk, and risk means there is a chance of failure.

As we examine our lives, we must face the reality that life is full of what I call "NSAs," or "Non-Safe Activities." Some activities in life are obviously on this list: skydiving, climbing Mount Everest, jumping the Grand Canyon like Evel Knievel, and apparently riding a bike. However, these are not the NSAs I am talking about. The things I speak of are far more practical and far scarier.

Friendship is a "Non-Safe Activity"

Marriage is a "Non-Safe Activity"

Raising children

Starting a new business

Planting a church

Attending a church for the first time

Serving someone in need

Sharing with someone about the hope you have in Jesus

Grieving with someone who has experienced loss

Giving advice from your mistakes

Dreaming

Hoping

Loving

Not one of these is safe. Each comes with tremendous risk.

This list could go on and on with everyday activities. Not only are these actions a part of our daily rhythm, but they require a commitment that cannot be faked. We must put our full self into these activities. And anytime we put our full self into something, there is a chance we will fall—hard. So I ask you again: How will you live with the risk of life and fear that comes with falling?

You can choose to live safe and reserved or secure and ridiculous.

I believe that the reality and acceptance of the revelation that God Chose Me can produce a life that is fully aware of the risk that awaits yet chooses to live secure and ridiculous. What do I mean by ridiculous? I am not talking about a sporadic and ill-thought life. No, I am speaking of the ridiculousness we see laced throughout the Scriptures and the life of Jesus—a willingness to obey God and love others no matter the optics.

A security and ridiculousness that has you build a boat when it isn't even raining yet.

A security and ridiculousness that has you move your entire legacy and family because Yahweh said He was going to give you children and you're way too old to have kids.

A security and ridiculousness that has you fight a giant with a slingshot while an entire army of trained warriors is cowering behind you.

A security and ridiculousness that has you stand up to a tyrant king to do what is right and save your people.

A security and ridiculousness that has you leave your family business and follow a rabbi you just met.

JESUS IS NOT SAFE

Friend, I have an announcement. If you decide to follow Jesus of Nazareth and if you decide to be courageous enough to believe the fact that He chose you, you are not safe—at least not in the way people define safety. In fact, it would be most accurate to say our savior is not safe.

Jesus did not live safe. He spent three years of ministry traveling to neighboring towns, stirring the pot. He wasn't a troublemaker, but He felt compelled to challenge the unhealthy religiosity of those in charge. He did everything but live safe and reserved. Jesus was incredibly secure in His identity and yet lived a ridiculous life.

He fed five thousand people with two fish and five loaves. He told people who had never walked to stand up. He asked men who had been rejected to be the most influential leaders of His mission. He barely had a home, and He lived as a nomad. And then He was murdered for His message, and His closest friends were murdered for the same belief. Yet somehow, many people today have created this politically correct, whitewashed Jesus who asks us to do only normal, safe, easy things. But Jesus called His followers to "take up their cross and follow [Him]" (Matthew 16:24, NIV). Jesus's message and Jesus's people have always been marked by a level of ridiculousness. Every other page of the Bible features some ridiculously underqualified individual being asked to do some ridiculously imposing thing.

This is the track record of God. He is constantly calling us *out* of safety, *out* of our security. Out of the shadows and the boxes we create to protect ourselves. I mean, Jesus asked one of His best friends to step out of a boat and into a hurricane on the sea! How can we read these kinds of stories and expect that what He asks us to do would make sense and involve no risk? Our savior is not safe, nor is the life He calls us to live.

You were not created to pursue a life of safety and security. You were created to do the impossible. To break molds and patterns. To turn the world upside down with a confidence and fire that is not concerned with what looks acceptable. You were not meant to live shy, scared, and safe. You were meant to have a spirit that looks for the impossible and expects God to show up. When you truly believe that you have been chosen by God there is a security that envelops your soul and begins to ignite a trust in Him that does not look for the safest route. You stand up in the face of doubt and insecurity and you declare, "With man this is impossible, but with God all things are possible" (Matthew 19:26, NIV). You stand up to injustice and say, "Whether or not my God saves me, I will not bow" (see Daniel 3:18). You live like the twelve misfits Jesus chose to follow Him during His three years of ministry. They did not have all the answers, but they were willing to look ridiculous.

Are you willing to sacrifice your safety to look silly for your savior?

It can be so easy to become concerned with being seen as cool, collected, and calculated that that we end up confining ourselves to a small, safe life. This is why we must find our security and worth in Christ alone. We cannot be obsessed with what people think while also be committed to following Christ. We cannot simultaneously maintain appearances and change the world for Jesus. In this walk, you will at some point have to make a clear decision, a line in the sand. A moment when you decide the life you want most is more important than a fleeting moment. It may not be the popular thing but will lead to peace, power, and ultimately your purpose.

Cool or Christ?

You cannot have casual sex and maintain clarity of mind and heart.

You cannot try to keep up with every person you follow and be a good steward of your money.

You cannot be on TikTok infinite hours a day and have peace.

You cannot binge-watch TV shows about adultery and extra-marital affairs and have a healthy thought life in your marriage.

You cannot raise godly kids while trying to be super cool in front of the other parents.

You cannot reach out and invite others to a life-changing church service if you're worried about whether they will think you're weird.

You can't do both. You gotta pick. Pause. Let me say this: You can. You can be split. You can live halfway in and halfway out. The only problem is you don't gain on either side! Do you want to be safe or follow Jesus?

You can live a reserved, protected, predictable life, or you can follow this wild Man from Nazareth as He travels from city to city on a mission from heaven. Which do you want? A small, safe life or a big, secure life?

As much as it is up to me, the Metcalf house is going to live on the edge. I am going to live with what my friend would call crazy faith.[1] I'm going to believe that my God really can do anything. I will not let one moment of fear define my story. I will not let one moment of failure be the end of me. I will continue to believe that God can do anything! I will live secure and ridiculous!

I am going to speak in tongues, pray for miracles, build the local church, be kind, believe in redemption, assume the best, and *ride my bike*!

What does this look like in your life?

It's Time to Live

Maybe you've stopped dreaming of a future because it seems like you missed your moment. I encourage you to get a journal and write down the life you envision and then take it a step further—tell somebody.

Maybe you have stopped making new friends because of who left you. Today, make a decision to get out of your comfort zone and introduce yourself to that person at school or work.

Maybe you have settled for joining the family business when you know there's more in you. You need to have a conversation with your family letting them know that you love and respect them, and you need to move on.

Maybe you have stopped believing for healing because of the doctor's report. Start praying and proclaiming what you know your God can do.

Maybe you've stopped praying for that one person because they seem too far gone. Invite them to church with you and see what God might do.

Maybe you've settled for an average marriage, but what if the remaining years could be your best yet?

Maybe you've been stuck in a mediocre mindset. Why don't you break it and decide to become the best you—for you. Perhaps you've stopped dreaming of where your ideas could go. Take the time to make a list of places you would love to see your work and start moving toward it.

Do you feel crazy? Do you feel like it would be insane to even speak your dreams out loud? Maybe you're worried about what will happen if you start moving toward your dream and nothing happens. Friend, what if you take a step toward your dream and something *does* happen? What if you are the first person in your family to break the pattern? What if you are the first from your city to make a difference? What if it works? What if it goes better than you expect? What if the God of the universe chose you and has a plan that is bigger than you could ever imagine? What if He wants to do something you could never take credit for? What if you go down in history as one of "those" people who were crazy enough to believe in the God of the universe, and He uses your life to turn the world upside down.

To help in your choice of how you are living your life, ask yourself these two questions: *What if?* and *Why not?* One of my favorite hoopers, Russ Westbrook, has made "Why not?" his life motto. "Why not?" Why not you? Why not now? What do you have to lose? Appearance, popularity, safety? What do you have to gain? Joy, hope, a new life? What if it works, and why not you? My prayer is that beyond your mistakes, beyond the risk of life, you would wake up every day with an unshakable confidence to face the day and say: "I'm not afraid to live" and "I'm not afraid to die."

Chapter 11

HE CHOSE . . . ME?

You did not choose me, but I chose you and appointed you so that
you might go and bear fruit.
—Jesus, John 15:16, NIV

My wife and I have only ever had one argument. Are you impressed? Worried? Let me share part of this argument:

Me: I'm sorry.

Abby: I don't believe you.

Me: *(In a more condescending tone)* I'm sorry . . .

Abby: I still do not believe you.

Me: *(Full send rude)* Cool, you don't have to believe me. I'm
sorry. I said it.

Before you jump to any conclusions, let me tell you the whole
truth. It is true that we have had one argument, but it would be
more accurate to say that we have had one argument one thousand times. I may be a young man, but I have learned that most
arguments boil down to the same issue. The topic changes, the
season changes, but the core of the frustration or tension never

really changes. People are constantly working and learning how to grow through their weaknesses that keep them in the same argument. The goal, at least for our marriage, is not that we never argue. I think arguing can be a sign of a healthy marriage if—and this is a big if—*you learn how to argue well.* It was in our first year of marriage that I discovered what our ongoing argument and challenge would be. We were in the middle of a heated discussion and Abby said these words to me: "Charles, it's not what you're saying; it's how you are saying it."

Over the years, I have come to realize that tone is everything. You can say "I'm sorry" in a way that clearly states, "I am not sorry at all, and I am only saying sorry to end the conversation." Or you can say I'm sorry in a tone that communicates regret and remorse and a desire for reconciliation. It's the same words but with a different spirit. I want to be sure that as we are building this posture for *God Chose Me,* we keep the right spirit. When you wake up in the morning and you choose to believe, confess, own, and live out the revelation "God Chose Me," the power is not just in what you say but how you say it.

The statement "God Chose Me" should encourage and develop a posture of humility, not pride. Gratitude, never an attitude. Reverence, not arrogance.

At the core of this message must be a deep awareness of one's weakness, fragility, and even depravity. When it comes to living a "God Chose Me" life, you must understand the power of "and."

YES, AND . . .

Have you ever gotten a reverse compliment? Though you may have never heard it coined that way, you've likely received one. Perhaps somebody said, "You're so amazing, but . . ." or, "I love that outfit, but do you think maybe . . ." Whatever kind comment they offered is completely negated by a three-letter word: *but.* I have learned through conversation and counsel that a more mature form of language is to depict your intentions by using the word *and,* not *but.*

For example, "You are doing a great job, and you still have some room to grow."

"That was a really good presentation, and I still have some questions."

"That dress is beautiful, and it makes your butt look big." (Which may or may not be a problem depending on who you ask . . . right?)

This may seem like a small detail; however, our ability to embrace the "and" is an essential tool in the hand of a believer. In fact, without the power of "and," you will never fully understand God.

God is not grace but then truth. He is grace *and* truth. He is not just but sometimes merciful. He is both just *and* merciful at the same time. He is Alpha *and* Omega. The Beginning *and* the End. He is *both and.*

It is important to embrace our "and."

God Chose Me, And . . .

I have found that this word *and* can be a powerful tool to remind myself who I am and where I am! You are chosen, yes, *and* God could have chosen anyone else.

You have been forgiven, *and* you have done nothing to deserve it.

When you begin to reflect and comprehend your "and," it produces an extreme sense of gratitude that changes the way you handle the fact that you are chosen. And ultimately it produces a posture of humility and reverence.

We must ask God to help us grow in humility and reverence. If we are not careful, the very message that is laced with the grace, mercy, and kindness of God can get twisted to become an excuse for arrogance and, quite frankly, a spirit that's the exact opposite of our savior's. It is the work of the believer to humbly live in the tension between the courage and confidence that comes from being chosen by God and the self-awareness that none of us deserve God's choosing. We are all—every one of us—equally unqualified to be chosen by God. Confidence and humility need not compete with each other, and when we truly understand that God has chosen us, we will gradually and simultaneously grow in both.

Too Good to Be True

Have you ever heard something that sounded way too wild to be true? Maybe your friend told a crazy story while you were out at lunch? Or maybe you got an email saying you had won fifteen million dollars only to realize you were being scammed by some African Prince. One day I was scrolling on social media, and I came across this reel of some of the most unbelievable information I had ever heard. It was a list of historical events that took place at the same time. Here are a few of my favorites:

> Wooly mammoths were walking the earth when the pyramids were being built.

> The Titanic sank the same year that Oreos were introduced in the United States.

> Queen Elizabeth and Marilyn Monroe were the same age.

> Abraham Lincoln could have sent a fax to the samurai.

Rosa Parks could've watched the movie *Shrek* in theaters.

Oxford University is hundreds of years older than the Aztec Empire.

Crazy, right? I am not sure why, but the idea that wooly mammoths were walking about while *The Prince of Egypt* was being made . . . blows my mind! Okay, so maybe that's not true, but my point is, there are some facts that simply seem too good to be true.

When it comes to being chosen by God, there are two paths in front of you. Though these two paths are rooted in the same emotion, they are displayed in two very different attitudes. It's natural that we could feel the overwhelming sense of inferiority that comes with believing "I am chosen by God." I can spiral into why I shouldn't or can't or am not the best choice. It is this self-awareness of my weakness that drives me into a selfish shame cycle. I question myself and my abilities and begin to talk myself out of what I previously believed to be true. From there my words and actions start to align, and I slowly go from living ready to living in a constant state of retreat. Instead of being confident in the fact that God Chose Me, I am insecure. And instead of living with the boldness and ridiculousness we spoke of in the previous chapter, I begin to step down and step back. You see, the challenge we all face is what we do with our weakness.

Our awareness of our weakness can either lead to a retreat from God or a reverence for God.

WHAT WILL YOU DO WITH YOUR WEAKNESS?

When we get stuck in the shame cycle of our weakness, it pulls us away from God and into our own emotions. We lose sight of His greatness and power and instead focus on our weakness and pain. I shift from ready to running. Perhaps you've had a season where you felt ready for what was in front of you. You were confident, secure, prepared, and it seemed like everything was going your way. Then everything changed and you went from ready to running. Running from calling, running from purpose, running from relationships, running from the very things you were created to do. If you have felt this way, you are not alone. This is the human condition and even people in Scripture experienced it.

SAUL'S SHORT STORY

In the Scriptures, we find the story of a man named Saul, the first king of Israel. Though God had made it clear that He did not want the children of Israel to have a king, because of comparison, the children of Israel desired to be like the other nations who had a visible king. God warned them that they would not like it; however, they wanted it their way, so God conceded. The prophet Samuel was tasked with anointing the king, and the Bible tells us he found a young man who stood head and shoulders above everyone else. But from the moment he was chosen, Saul second-guessed who he was.

Saul told Samuel, "Am I not a Benjamite, from the smallest tribe of Israel, and is not my clan the least of all the clans of the tribe of Benjamin? Why do you say such a thing to me?" (1 Samuel 9:21).

From the moment he was chosen, Saul's weakness led.

Fast-forward to the day that Saul was to be presented as king. It had already been decided by God and with Samuel, and now it was time to announce it to the people. The Bible tells us that Saul was missing and was finally found hiding among the baggage. Now, that will preach all by itself, but it illustrates a key point.

Whenever we find ourselves stuck in shame and insecurity, focusing on our own issues, we shrink ourselves, and shrinking causes us to retreat and hide beneath things that ultimately cannot protect us. The same is true for Saul. His insecurities forced him to hide. Granted, we all have insecurities. The question that can shift our perspective is: What will you do with your insecurities? Will you hide and retreat? Or will you lean into the holiness of the God who has chosen you?

Sadly, throughout Saul's entire story, he never moves past this insecurity. He ends up ruining his relationship with David because he is so insecure. Eventually his insecurity comes out as rage and anger as he hunts David in order to kill him.

RETREAT OR REVERENCE?

When you focus on yourself, the only result is a spiral of insecurity and shame that pulls you away from God. This could explain why some of you struggle to make progress. You repeatedly find yourself spiraling in the thoughts of why you can't or what you should have done. It is this cycle that keeps us stuck. However, when you turn your focus from the power of your weakness to the power of your God, a unique shift happens. Instead of retreating from God, you develop a deep gratitude and reverence in your heart. You realize that your weaknesses not only qualify you to be used by God but they also become a source of humility in your life.

The journey toward living with confidence that God chose you comes with many emotions and challenges. One that has continually plagued my mind is that it all seems too good to be true. It's easy for me to believe that God would choose some people. In fact, it makes complete sense that there are certain types of people who are more qualified or prone to be chosen—but I am not on that list.

Some people just seem to have it all together. They are organized, calm, cool, and collected. They always make the right choice, and there is never a gap between their intention and their actions. They just seem to have all the pieces in their box, and they don't miss. I, on the other hand, am the opposite. I am inconsistent and constantly making mistakes, and I simply do not have what it seems everyone else has. It is this voice and confession that has played in my head and heart so many times. And the more I listen to this voice, the more I seem to talk myself out of the reality of being chosen. This is the unhealthiest part of my overwhelming insecurity. I retreat from God. However, there is an alternative.

There's a posture we can take that recognizes the power of "and."

I am called by God, and He could've chosen anybody.

I am insanely gifted, and I am equally as frail.

I am unique, and I am not better than.

I am *the* mother for these children, and I still get overwhelmed.

I have everything I need to be a good father, and I am nervous about how I will provide.

I love God, and I still have some questions.

God has used me, and He doesn't have to.

I believe, and I don't believe.

I am an addict, and I am breaking free.

I have come a long way, and I still need His grace every day.

Throughout my life, I have experienced many overwhelming moments. This book has been that for me, as I have flipped page after page, edit after edit. There are moments I am tempted to focus on myself, my weakness, my deficiencies. And every time I've done that, it has led me to a shame that retreats from God.

However, as I continued to persevere through the process of writing this book, I found myself pausing with deep emotion to say . . .

I can't believe He chose me.

Out of anyone who God could've given this message to, out of all the authors in the world, out of anyone on this planet, God Chose Me. For this moment, for this day, for this hour. For this message. For this chapter. For this sentence. I will not waste another day hesitating or apologizing for the fact that God Chose Me.

Friend, I pray you experience the deep gratitude of a moment like this daily. That you would pause long enough to look around at the blessings in your life and be honest with yourself. Honest enough to admit you couldn't have planned this. Honest enough to realize that no matter how organized you are, you aren't organized enough. To realize that every good thing in your life is a miracle. May you recognize how God has taken your mess and made a masterpiece, and may you say, "God Chose Me."

Chapter 12

GET UP, DONNIE!

The credit belongs to the man who is actually in the arena, whose face is marred by dust and sweat and blood, who strives valiantly; . . . who, at the best, knows, in the end, the triumph of high achievement, and who, at the worst, if he fails, at least he fails while daring greatly, so that his place shall never be with those cold and timid souls who knew neither victory nor defeat.
—Theodore Roosevelt, *"It Is Not the Critic Who Counts," Speech at the Sorbonne, 1910*

I s anyone else confused by the Bible? I know that may seem like a strange question for a book about being chosen by God, but I think it's important. In fact, it's so important that I've already begun writing my second book, which will be focused around some of the key questions from Scripture. I think it's easy to pretend you don't have questions. I have been reading the Bible since I was five years old and have taught it for the last twelve years, and I'm not sure if I have more answers or more questions. It is full of stories of triumph and failure. Full of heroes and villains—and many times they are one and the same. I have heard it almost perfectly articulated as not the story of God with man but the story of man with God. The reason the scriptures are so full of brokenness, pain, murder, vices, and so on is because that is who we are. It is a picture of humanity and God's unfailing plan for imperfect people. It is full of hope and joy, power and wisdom. Yet, amid all its power, there are moments where I find myself utterly confused at the content of this book, including anytime I have found myself reading the book of Job. If you are not familiar with it, let me take you on the stunning and confusing journey of Job.

THE BOOK OF JOB WAS A JOB

The book of Job opens with a wild scene:

> One day the angels came to present themselves before the LORD, and Satan also came with them. The LORD said to Satan, "Where have you come from?"
>
> Satan answered the LORD, "From roaming throughout the earth, going back and forth on it."
>
> Then the LORD said to Satan, "Have you considered my servant Job? There is no one on earth like him; he is blameless and upright, a man who fears God and shuns evil." (1:6–8, NIV)

Did you catch that? God is chilling in heaven, and the angels come to see Him and check in, and the devil just strolls in. Now at this point, some theologians differ on if it is actually Satan himself or a being named "the accuser." However, can you imagine it's like that guy who graduated from high school but has nothing better to do than hang around the school getting people in trouble. Satan walks in and God asks him what he's been up to, and Satan says, "Oh, you know, just roaming around doing my thang" (verse 7, my paraphrase). Then God does one of the most confusing and frustrating things I have ever seen in Scripture. He volunteers Job to the devil! He brings him up as though He is bragging to the devil, saying, "He's the best one I got!" This is where weak theology like "Good things happen to good people and bad things happen to bad people" goes flying out the window. Job is spoken of as God's most stand-up guy, which does not remove him from the fight but actually qualifies him for it.

Over its forty-two chapters, the book of Job is filled with a back-and-forth of trial, loss, disappointment with God, and grief.

In a shockingly short time, Job lost all his wealth, his livestock, his servants, and his ten children. He was then struck with painful boils all over his body. It is during this moment that we see Job and his community wrestle though some of the biggest and most honest questions on why suffering happens and what we deserve.

Job went from being one of the richest men to losing everything. His own wife suggested he curse God and die. But even at his lowest moment, he refused to break. "Job replied, 'You talk like a foolish woman. Should we accept only good things from the hand of God and never anything bad?' So in all this, Job said nothing wrong" (Job 2:10).

No matter who you are, at some point you will find yourself knocked down. Some questions to consider: Where do you find the strength to stand back up? Where do you find the source of hope to try again, even when you've failed? What keeps you from giving up? What pushes you to try again?

WHERE DO YOU GET YOUR STRENGTH?

I have learned that we all have different motivators for why we do what we do. For some, it's influence. For others, it's money. For still others, it's to prove someone wrong or the desperate search for love and acceptance. And for some, it is this deep inner drive to have impact. The question is not whether we have a source for our strength, but what that source is. When you are broken and empty and see no way out, what makes you get back up? What keeps you from throwing in the towel? Is it your commitment, your family, fear, hope? Your willpower? What is the engine that keeps you going?

The important thing to understand is that most of our motivators are not inherently bad. They are simply the tools we were given early in life. However, if we aren't careful, we will never upgrade from our juvenile ways to actual tools that serve us as we mature.

We all go through life with these broken mechanisms, trying to fuel ourselves for things that are far greater than we ever dreamed. As children, we tend to get back up because we simply believe we can try again. However, as we get older, time and failure rob us of the confidence we had. In our early twenties, we felt like the breakup wasn't a big deal because we still had time, but now we're in our late thirties and the risk of relationship is far too great for us to take another step. It was fine to fail when it was our first and we had nothing on the line. But now we have a family to feed and employees depending on us—failure is not an option. Where do we get the strength to keep going, find the tenacity to get back up after being knocked down time and time again?

Among the many blessings that come with believing "God Chose Me" is a deeper and more secure resilience.

Once you accept that God has chosen you, you discover a new source, a new motivator, a new engine for why you can get back up. If you embrace the revelation that God chose you, you will find a reservoir of resilience you didn't know you had.

I want to go back to Job's journey for a minute.

If I were Job, at some point I would have asked myself, *Why am I chosen? Why is this happening to me? Why, after doing the right thing over and over, do I keep experiencing loss after loss after loss?* In fact, Job did wrestle with these kinds of questions. Job had lived a blameless life, a life of integrity, purpose, generosity, and success, and yet he found himself experiencing the opposite of what it seems someone like this *should* experience. We assume that people who do good and work hard should be rewarded. And yet Job's family was taken. His money was taken. He was inflicted with horrible pain and suffering. All because he did the wrong thing? No, he did nothing wrong. In fact, Scripture says despite all his loss, he never sinned. This brings up the question, Why? Why did Job go through all of this? Why did God allow the devil to attack him? Why?

WHY ME, GOD?

There have been many times in my life when I've gotten stuck on why. Stuck on why God would allow something to happen to me. Stuck on why God would allow good things to happen to bad people. Stuck on why God would allow people who don't deserve it to experience horrific things. If you look around, you will see plenty of injustice and unexplainable hurt. And it makes us ask why.

In fact, as I was writing this book, some of my dearest friends in the world experienced the deepest and most confusing heartbreak I've ever witnessed. After years of trying, our dear friends finally became pregnant with a wonderful little boy named Ace. Our community exploded with joy at the thought of adding this little guy to our tribe. If anyone deserved to have the brightest and best pregnancy, it was these two. They are kind, strong, and the best auntie and uncle to everyone's kids, and they have fought like hell for a beautiful marriage and life together. Without going into all the details, we would soon find out that Baby Ace was facing serious complications. These issues became so severe that our friends had to relocate to Houston to prioritize their son's health. From that moment on, it was a battle. We were confident that God was going to do a miracle for that boy.

Friends, family, and thousands of people around the world began to pray and believe for Ace's healing.

We prayed like our lives depended on it.

We prayed with faith.

We prayed believing God would heal Ace.

And He did. Just not this side of eternity.

Ace James Davis went to be with Jesus after just a few short days on this earth.

Even now, as I sit writing this chapter months later, my eyes are filled with tears. I can't help but imagine what he would be like. How silly he would be and if I would've let him date one of my daughters one day. Ever since we lost Ace, I have found myself asking God, *Why?*

God, why didn't You heal him? Why did You let this happen? Why would You do this to Brie and Aaron? They're good people—don't You care about them? God, why? Were our prayers not enough? Did you not hear us? Why, God, why?

The truth is, I do not know why. I do not know why God didn't heal Ace on earth. In my opinion, having that little boy here with us was the only and best plan. But for some reason, it didn't go that way. Being honest, there are a lot of things about God I can't explain—why bad things happen to good people, why He doesn't heal everyone, or why life isn't as fair as we would want.

I don't know how or why you have been knocked down. I don't know why that family member abandoned you. I don't know why you didn't get accepted to that school even though you had all the grades and qualifications. I don't know why they left. I don't know why that person has not said they're sorry. But I want to offer you a challenge.

Instead of asking *why,* I want you to ask *what.*

We cannot control the why. As much as the human soul desires to know every answer and every detail, we simply cannot. We don't know why many things happen in this life or why we may find ourselves where we are. But among all of our questions, there is something we do have control over. We have control over what.

WHAT WILL YOU DO WITH YOUR WHY?

What if you took the question of why and moved it to the question of what?

What will you do with your next moment?

What will you do after you face unspeakable pain?

What will you do after they leave?

What will you do after you settle into the reality that you have lost your job?

What will you do after your plans fail?

What will you do—and where will you get the strength to do it?

My hope is to provide you with a better option, one that does not include comparing yourself or faking it till you make it. This option includes a genuine source of strength that does not come from your capability but from God's ability.

The *Oxford English Dictionary* defines resilience as "the capacity to withstand or to recover quickly from difficulties; toughness."[1] Resilience is something I believe we all want and admire. It's easy to look at warriors and athletes, those in business and in any successful sphere, and admire those who seem to get back up.

It's every *Rocky* movie we've ever seen. It is the grit to never give up. The question that lies before each one of us is, Why?

Why get back up? Why try again? Why take the risk of a relationship? Why reapply to that college? Why try church again? Why try God again? Why try to succeed when I have failed?

The truth is, if you do not have a strong enough why, you will never get back up.

I once heard Gail Hyatt say, "When you lose your why, you lose your way."

Whenever we are knocked down in life, it forces us to question our original motivating factors.

WHY DO YOU WANT IT?

Many of our motivations for why we do what we do are not very deep and, honestly, are sometimes quite vain. We wanted to get the job to make the money so we could show everyone else that we are worth something. We get the money, we get the job, we get the car—only to find out it's not what we needed. Then, slowly, we lose motivation; we lose hope. We realize that a life of money and influence is empty if we don't have relationships. We start to lose our why, and then we lose our way.

Maybe you want to be at the top of your sporting event. You want to be the best, so you practice harder than everyone else—

only to get to the top and realize it's empty. It did not fulfill the void inside of you. So what do you do? You lose hope. You wonder, *Why get back up if this isn't going to fulfill me?*

Maybe you're not in business and not an all-star athlete—maybe you're a single mother. You've worked your hardest to raise your kids to follow God, and you're doing your best. You work multiple jobs as you struggle to pay the bills, but things keep going wrong. You think to yourself, *If I've worked hard and it hasn't worked, why would it ever work?*

Why should you keep fighting?

The truth is, if you don't have a strong why, you'll never have the resilience to get back up. It is my conviction that the revelation "God Chose Me" is the strongest why for your resilience.

I CAN GET UP BECAUSE . . .

When you start to believe God chose you, it ignites your spirit with hope.

Because if God chose you, that means He has a plan, and if God has a plan, that means He knows the future. And if God knows the future, that means I can trust Him. And if I can trust Him, I can have hope. And if I can have hope, I can get back up.

You see, friend, because God chose you, you can get back up.

Because God chose you, you can try again.

Because God chose you, you can stand with your head held high.

I know you may feel tired of falling. I know you may feel tired of making mistakes. It's exhausting to try and then fail, but as long as you believe God chose you, there is hope for tomorrow. Lying within you is the seed of hope, and when you plant this seed in the soil of faith and expectation, you will be amazed at what God can do.

Job lost everything—those he loved, the things he had accumulated. But deep down in his soul, there was something that kept him—from cursing God and from abandoning his faith—and it was a real, powerful *why*.

Maybe you've been knocked down and you find yourself in the lowest moment. Maybe you feel like there's no hope to get up tomorrow. Maybe life is going well but you need faith to believe it all won't come crashing down. I believe you have everything you need to be resilient, and I want to present three reasons why you can get back up.

Number one, you owe it to you.

I know you're not perfect. I know you've made mistakes. Life hasn't gone exactly how you wanted it to, but you've come too far to come only this far. Look at what you've accomplished, how many habits you've changed, and all the hardships you've overcome. You owe it to yourself to see what tomorrow holds. You owe it to yourself to see what you're capable of. You owe it to yourself to see what would happen if you try again. You may not be where you want to be, but you definitely aren't where you used to be. Which is proof of the power you hold.

I know you have real fear. I know you fell hard, but the truth is, you were close. You almost had it. I know the shame is telling you right now: You're so far gone that there's no hope. But the truth is, trying means you're close. Trying means you're in the fight, and, friend, you owe it to you to try one more time.

Number two, you owe it to them.

THEY HAVE TO SEE YOU STAND

You owe it to those who are watching. The reason we all love the *Rocky* movies is not because we believe Rocky is a real boxer or that we really want him to stand up and beat Drago. We love Rocky because when we watch him stand up in the last round, it makes us feel like we can stand up in our last round. Whether you realize it or not, there are people watching your life. There are people who are seeing how you raise your children, how you run your business, how you pursue your dreams, and how you navigate school. The confidence you carry and the example you set. They're watching how you navigate pain and hardship. How you respond to suffering. When you stand up, it gives them the hope to stand up.

You don't have to be perfect. You don't have to have it all figured out. It doesn't have to be pretty as you scramble to your feet. You can stand up with your nose bleeding and your knees shaking. But when you stand up, the crowd takes a deep breath. The world stands at attention. There are those who see you, and it fills them with strength.

Not only do you owe it to you and to them, but the third reason you can get back is up is that you owe it to Him.

He Came Out so You Could Stand Up

The truth is, you can stand up because Christ got up. The Bible tells us that Jesus was the only perfect sacrifice that ever could have been. When Jesus was on His way to follow the will of His Father, He paused in the Garden of Gethsemane. In this garden, He was so anxious that the Bible tells us He began to sweat blood. This is not just metaphor or analogy; there is an actual physiological response that the body has under extreme distress where the pores actually sweat blood.[2] Jesus was so nervous, so full of distress, so human. He prayed a vulnerable prayer in the garden: "Father, if you are willing, take this cup from me; yet not my will, but yours be done" (Luke 22:42, NIV). He was essentially asking God if there was any other way to accomplish His mission besides dying on the cross, but no matter what, Jesus was determined to submit to God's will.

Then He stood up and prepared to go to His death. He was beaten beyond recognition, was hung on a cross, and died. He was down for three days. The world seemed cold and dark. The disciples lost hope. Everything they had worked for had been knocked down. Yet early on Sunday morning, two women arrived at the tomb to pay their respects, but Jesus was not there. The angel told them, "He has risen, just as he said" (Matthew 28:6). The women ran to tell the men. (It is worth noting that women were the first to proclaim the gospel.) And in this moment, Jesus gave hope to all humanity. He stood up from the thing one never stands up from: death. He is resilient, even in death.

The reason you can have resilience is not because you're perfect. It's not because life is easy. It's not because things are always going to go your way. You can be resilient because of the resurrection of Jesus. The Bible says that the same power that raised Christ from the dead lives inside of you (see Romans 8:11).

And if Jesus had the power to stand up out of the tomb, you have the power to stand up too—today, tomorrow, and every day.

GET UP, DONNIE

Some of you have been waiting for me to explain the title of this chapter. "Get up, Donnie" is one of my favorite lines from the movie *Creed*. If you haven't seen it, you've probably been living under a rock. Even so, I'll take a moment to explain it to you.

Creed is the continuation of the *Rocky* movies. Apollo Creed was once Rocky's archnemesis but ended up becoming his best friend. Apollo was tragically killed in a fight against Drago. *Creed* picks up with the story of Apollo's son Adonis (Donnie). Adonis has had a tattered past. He's been searching for identity and purpose. Somehow, he finds himself in the ring, just like his father. There's a moment in the first *Creed* film when Donnie is having his first chance at a title fight. He has overcome the odds, he has fought against the naysayers, and he has come to the biggest fight of his life. In true, dramatic, *Rocky* fashion, it comes down to the final moments, and with one fell swoop, Donnie gets knocked down. He's lying on the ground. The room goes silent, and memories start to flash through his mind.

Him in juvenile.

His father boxing.

His father lying on the ground.

You can hear Donnie's heartbeat as the faint sound gets lower and lower.

In the background, the love of his life yells his name as everything seems to fade away, and three words come piercing through his memory.

"Get up, Donnie!"

He gasps a deep breath and stands up.

He walks to his corner where his coach asks him his name. With every ounce of passion, he yells, "Creed!" The question is deeper than a mere examination of Donnie's fitness to continue fighting. It is a question of identity. It is more than about memory. It is a moment. A moment to show the world that Donnie knows who he is and that he is not going anywhere. Donnie decides that he is not ashamed of his last name—he is proud of it. He's not going to hide from it anymore. He's going to stand up and fight as his own person. But more than that, Donnie embraces who he is and who he belongs to. From that moment on, he begins to fight with everything in him.

Don't Forget the Name You Carry

Just like Donnie, you have a decision to make: Will you embrace your name? Will you embrace whose name is on you? I'm not talking about the name of your father or the name of the person who adopted you or even your mother's name. The name that resides on you is the name of Christ, the name of Jesus. His is the name that you bear, and He is the reason you stand back up.

I'm not sure what tomorrow holds. I'm not sure what challenges you're facing. I'm not sure how many times you've been knocked down. But what I do know is there's a power within you that is stronger than the pain you're experiencing. There's a power within you that the Bible says is stronger than anything we could face on this planet. So when you find yourself knocked down, when you find yourself questioning why, when you find yourself stuck in the middle of a situation that does not make sense and you wonder why you should get up now, I want you to remember first that you owe it to yourself. You can stand up. You're stronger than you think. There's more in you than you think. You also owe it to them. There's someone watching you, and your stand gives them strength. And lastly, you owe it to Him. Jesus. You can be resilient because of the Resurrection.

You've got the grit to get up.

And I'm gonna say this in the kindest and most challenging way: It's time to get up. It's time to stop lying down. It's time to stop questioning why and start taking responsibility for what you're gonna do. It's time to become the version of yourself you know is possible. Stop waiting on the permission or right people.

It's time to do what only you can do. To step up and fight for what really matters to you. Who you are and what is inside of you is worth fighting for. You may have been knocked down, but you can get back up.

The bell has rung. The crowd stands at attention. The time has come for you to fight because God chose you. You can be resilient.

Chapter 13

ALL I NEED IS A MEMORY

*I wish there was a way to know you're in "the good old days," be-
fore you've actually left them.*
                    —Andy Bernard, The Office

It's still so vivid in my mind. My mom, my cousin, and I were riding in a red convertible. Looking back, I'm not sure where we got
the car from, but the wind was blowing and we were all screaming
these lyrics:

Come on, ride the train, hey, ride it
Come on, ride the train, hey, ride it

It was "C'Mon n' Ride It (The Train)" by Quad City DJ's.

Now let me pause and say I have no idea why I was listening to
this song at such a young age. I definitely had no concept of what
the lyrics were about. To me, they were riding a party train to who
knows where and I was in! Anyway, I vividly remember the sound
of a train they sampled, the conductors horn, and the beat. I recall
laughing as my mom drove with one hand on the wheel and one

hand in the air, acting as the conductor of this party we were having in our red convertible. That moment was forever locked in my soul. Full of so much light and joy.

To this day, whenever I hear those lyrics, I am instantly transported back to that moment, with almost the exact emotions.

GOD WAS IN HIS BAG WHEN HE MADE OUR BRAINS

A memory is one of the most powerful things we possess as humans. It's crazy and overwhelming to me how God designed our brains.

The human brain is one of the most complex and powerful organs in the body, containing approximately eighty-six billion neurons that communicate with each other through electrical and chemical signals.[1] These neurons form intricate networks, enabling everything from basic motor functions to complex thoughts, emotions, and decision-making processes. The speed at which the brain operates is remarkable—neurons can fire signals at speeds up to 268 miles per hour (431 km/h).[2] Each neuron can connect to thousands of other neurons through synapses, creating trillions of connections, or neural pathways, which allow the brain to process vast amounts of information in milliseconds.[3] This rapid firing underlies our ability to react to stimuli almost instantaneously, think critically, and store and recall memories, making the brain not only incredibly fast but also capable of extraordinary adaptability and learning.

One memory can change your future.

Here's what I want you to hold on to:

A memory triggers your focus.

Your focus triggers a feeling.

Feeling produces fruit.

Focus–Feeling–Fruit

Let's imagine that you recall the first time you played at recess, when you walked out to the playground and awkwardly stood there looking for a friend. A friend yelled across the yard, and you ran toward the monkey bars. You began to play tag as you chased each other up and down the slide and around the swing. Suddenly, as you are navigating this memory, you begin to focus on the joys of being a kid. That focus turns into a feeling of nostalgia. You think on how much time has passed, how much has happened, and how much things have changed. You begin to feel how different things are and how much you miss that time of your life.

From that feeling comes fruit. Maybe it's the desire to pick a new hobby or to call an old friend. No matter the memory, it always leads to focus, and feeling, which leads to fruit.

This fruit is a product—something that results from whatever you're thinking about. In the memory of the playground, your focus on how things have changed produced the fruit of nostalgia. Maybe you begin to miss some of those old friends. Maybe you wonder where they are. Maybe you even look them up on Facebook to see how their lives have progressed. What started as a memory produced a focus, which produced a feeling, which produced fruit.

Lying dormant within your memories could be the fruit, the future, and the fuel you have been desperately searching for in order to live the life God called you to live. But before we spend time remembering, I need to address the inverse: forgetting.

All of us have experienced pain and hardship, as we spoke about previously. We often try to forget the past, forget the things we miss, forget the mistakes we've made, forget the embarrassing clothes we wore—forget. Most of us prefer to focus on the future. In some regards, this is beneficial. It does no good to focus on things you cannot change. However, in all this forgetting, I fear that we are being robbed of some of the most important fuel God gives believers: the power to remember. To remember the times when it wasn't perfect, to remember the ups and downs, to remember the past. You see, if you tap into the power of your memory, you can find the fuel, the fruit, and the focus for a future of confidence and contentment. In fact, when God was leading the children of Israel to their promised land, He made memory a core facet of their entire civilization.

SET THE STONES

In Joshua 4, we witness an interesting moment with the children of Israel. They had just experienced yet another impossible miracle. As they carried the ark of the covenant, which symbolized God's presence, they witnessed God part the water and they crossed through the Jordan River on dry ground. This was not the first time God had made a way. He did the same thing with the Red Sea as they were escaping four hundred years of slavery in Egypt.

Scripture says that when they had crossed the Jordan, Joshua asked one man from each tribe to grab a stone, according to God's command. They were to set these stones up to represent the twelve tribes of Israel. Then God gave a very specific instruction.

> When the whole nation had finished crossing the Jordan, the Lord said to Joshua, "Choose twelve men from among the people, one from each tribe, and tell them to take up twelve stones from the middle of the Jordan, from right

where the priests are standing, and carry them over with you and put them down at the place where you stay tonight."

So Joshua called together the twelve men he had appointed from the Israelites, one from each tribe, and said to them, "Go over before the ark of the LORD your God into the middle of the Jordan. Each of you is to take up a stone on his shoulder, according to the number of the tribes of the Israelites, to serve as a sign among you. In the future, when your children ask you, 'What do these stones mean?' tell them that the flow of the Jordan was cut off before the ark of the covenant of the LORD. When it crossed the Jordan, the waters of the Jordan were cut off. These stones are to be a memorial to the people of Israel forever." (verses 1–7, NIV)

God mandated that His people create a pattern of remembering who God is and what He had done. This pattern is not just for the ancient children of Israel. It should be a practice that we all carry with us daily.

WHEN I THINK ABOUT JESUS

The title of this chapter finds its origins in the genius that is my friend Roosevelt Stewart. There was one Sunday when he began to sing "All I need is a memory," and it literally sent me into a whole sanctified fit. When we pause to remember what God has done, we are intentionally taking a moment to stop and look back on the goodness of God. During the many distractions of our lives, we often fail to realize the faithfulness and history we have with God. When we feel stuck in our current situation, it can be easy to forget how God has consistently made a way time and time again. The children of Israel were commanded to produce a physical representation of the miracle that God had performed. As they did this physical act, they were forced to remember what God had done for them. This was meant to spark gratitude, joy, and hope not only in their hearts but in the hearts of the children who would come after them.

There is an untapped resource of hope, joy, expectation, and faith that lies dormant in the recesses of your memory. You may have worked hard to forget your past, and I am by no means asking you to dig up old wounds. However, I do believe that if you were to review the history of your life, you would recognize God's track record of faithfulness. As we reflect on our lives, we will start to remember and our souls will begin to feel hope and light, knowing that God always comes through.

There's a song we used to sing in my childhood church, and we still sing it today at Transformation.

When I think about Jesus
What He's done for me . . .
I could dance, dance, dance, dance, dance, dance, dance . . . [4]

(I bet some of y'all just took off running.)

When I look back over my life and see how God made a way even when I was so depressed I couldn't even go outside, even when I was stuck in crippling fear and my heart was broken, my soul is ignited with the flame of faith to believe that if He did it then, He can definitely do it again.

That is the word I have for you in this chapter.

If He did it then, He can do it again.

If He set you free once, He can do it again.

If He healed you once, He can do it again.

If He's been your strength once, He can do it again.

If He's opened the door once, He can do it again.

If He has been your provider once, He can do it again.

If He has healed you once, He can do it again.

He is a way-making, chain-breaking, mind-restoring, heart-healing, body-transforming, marriage-mending, purpose-giving, all-powerful God. How do I know? Because I remember every time He's done those things in my life.

Just Stop and Remember

I encourage you to stop right now. Before you move past this point in the book, I believe some of you will find the power you need in this moment. Put the book down. Take just a moment. Maybe on your phone, in a notebook, or with a friend. Just stop and remember every time He's come through. Everything He has done. Times you were afraid. Times you didn't know where to go or what to do. When you felt hopeless and hurt. The times your soul said, *We will never make it past this.* I am convinced it won't be long before you find yourself looking up with hope and possibly even shouting:

"If He's done it once, He can do it again!"

Chapter 14

MY FRIENDS SAVED MY LIFE

If you hang with nine broke friends, you are bound to be the tenth one.

—Granny Estelle

I love my parents. I have the best parents anyone could ask for. As I have gotten older, I have come to deeply appreciate what they've done for me. They intentionally created a beautiful life for me and my brother. They married young, had kids young, and so, in a desire to build the best life for us, my dad worked his way up the corporate ladder, getting promotion after promotion. He was always the youngest, the newest—sometimes the blackest—but he always excelled. These jobs led us to different cities and different states, some close to family and some far. With a mix of career, calling, and always faith, my parents followed God and followed the opportunities that would help our family flourish. One result of our moving was that my brother and I went to many different schools.

For me, changing schools was always a mixed bag of emotions. On one hand, I was excited to be the new and mysterious kid. On the other hand, I was nervous to have to reset and restart making friends. But with all the times we moved, all the new teams I joined, I became good at making friends.

Each new school felt like a new opportunity to reinvent myself. At some schools, I was the cool, weird, artsy kid. At other schools, I sold out to sports. At one school I even tried to change my name. It lasted for about a week before I went back to Charles.

I credit that season of life to shaping much of who I am. I learned how to communicate clearly, build trust, and relate to a lot of different people—skills I use every single day.

Among all the beautiful lessons I learned through that season, there is one downside that represents something I have continued to work on. Though I learned how to make friends quickly, I was also guarded. I made a lot of friends, but our friendships only went so far. My logic was that in a few months or a few years, I would move. So what was the point of getting to know people deeply if I would soon be gone? It was my own defense mechanism. This was my way of avoiding getting hurt. However, as I entered my adult years and even marriage, I realized I had work to do. I was settled and had time to form relationships, but for some reason, I couldn't get past a certain point.

A List of All My Friends

As I look back over my life, I remember the many friends I've had. (Warning: I am about to list a ton of random people you have never met. It matters and it doesn't. Proceed accordingly.)

Early on, I had a friend named Samir. We connected over fashion, music, and basketball. I had another friend named Spencer. He was the kid with the really big house and the really nice family. We also played basketball together. There was Nathan, the artsy kid. He could draw really well. He wore quirky clothes and his jeans were ripped—so cool. He also had a Great Dane, and I thought that was awesome. Then I moved and made another group of friends, which included Brady and Payne. These people shaped a lot of my high school years. They were friends in my youth group, and we went on mission trips together, snuck out of houses together, and got our first cars together.

Then during my senior year, I moved to Oklahoma. At first I didn't have any friends, but then I met one dude in my neighborhood. He was a couple of years younger than me, but we became the best of friends. We bonded because we were both new kids who did not want to live where we were. We were kind of rude to everybody, but that was our thing.

I never had a lot of friends, but I always had the friends I needed when I needed them. As I've gotten older, that has continued to be true. When I got my first job at PacSun, I had a friend named Rick. He was the manager, and he was wild. He had the coolest tattoos and was the most fun person to work for.

Then I worked at my first ministry job as an intern and had a friend named Daniel. Daniel wasn't technically my boss, but I really wanted to do what he did, so I followed him around, and he showed me the ropes.

I also had a friend named Wes. He was the older cool guy and seemed like the only person I could relate to in that season of life. Then I moved again.

There were Chris, Michael, and Jeremy.

Then I made a friend named Abby. I ended up marrying her. Period.

Adrian and Asia are the funniest people you could imagine. We could laugh harder than anybody else. I have a tattoo of their first son's initials on my arm.

Parker, Sarah, Matt, Kaleo, Issac, Taylor, Kelton, Justice aka Juice—I love you and think of you often. Micah aka Noodle Boy.

CEO of ZEAL and original Italian mobster. Zach, owner of the best brand in the world: Basketcase.

Justin. Telsha. Shout-out to Baby Shepard.

Filmore and Cait: The best pastors ever, and I must admit that Filmore is a cold hooper.

Mariah and Jake: best-dressed friends.

Tyler and Josie. Tyler saved my life, and Josie is the *best*. Love you both so much.

Chandler and Hannah: They are absolute fools in the best way.

Aden, Yani

Amberly, Will (Barbie and Ken)

Heather, Angela

Will and Kaylee Huckleberry

Ty and Dr. Daly Doodles

Ava, Charlie, Roman, Michael aka DOCTOR

Michiah, Erin

Brooke and Anler (best cycling friend ever)

G MOB: creative genius.

Chan and Lori: Shout out to my real-life brother and sister, who are my favorite people.

Carl, Laura (BEEEEBOOOOOOP)

Mike, Natalie: King and the Queen

Brie, Aaron: BFFL

If I keep going, I will run out of space. Also, if I didn't mention your name, it's because I don't know you or I missed it while writing this section at three in the morning.

You may have read this list and thought, *Okay, Charles, we get it. You have a lot of friends.*

And you would be right—I have a lot of friends. But in another sense, I don't have a lot of friends. These friends have been spaced out over different seasons, different interests, different callings.

The Right People at the Right Time

God has graciously supplied me with friends who have supported me, encouraged me, and helped me follow Jesus. He has brought the right people at the right time when I needed them. I have not had a ton of friends, but I have always had the right friends.

The same may be true in your life. When I started writing this chapter, I had the perspective that I haven't had many friends. But as I began to remember, my mind was flooded with so many memories, so much laughter, so many hardships, pain, and moments that connected me with people I never thought I would relate to. And yet we became dear friends. These friendships have been crucial to navigating life changes and hard times. What connected me to my friends was different but always right in every season.

The message of God choosing me is not one of isolation but relationships. This book is titled *God Chose Me*, but it could also be *God Chose Us*.

A common misconception when it comes to following Jesus is that it's about individualism, but that could not be further from the truth.

It Can't Be Just You and Jesus

Many people today sum up Christianity with, "It's just me and Jesus."

Usually what that means is we have failed to steward our relationships properly—they have fallen apart, and now we use "me and Jesus" as an excuse to do our own thing and get checked by no one. But just you and Jesus is not how Jesus intended it. In fact, that is the very opposite of what He desires and how Jesus Himself lived His life.

If anybody had an excuse to not have friends—if anybody technically didn't need anybody—it would have been Jesus. But He chose to live in community. In fact, He chose twelve wild kids. That's right—many scholars suggest that most of the disciples were in their late teens to early twenties. In fact, some would argue that the oldest was Peter, who was around twenty years old when he started following Jesus, since people didn't have to pay temple tax until that age,[1] and Peter is the only disciple mentioned in Scripture who did this (see Matthew 17:24–27). Regardless of the disciples' ages, Jesus chose a ragtag group of people to be His best friends, to do life with, and to share His most vulnerable moments with. He refused to live in isolation. He constantly invited people to be with Him.

In addition to Jesus's example, I am reminded of the scripture that says, "Though one may be overpowered, two can defend themselves. A cord of three strands is not quickly broken" (Ecclesiastes 4:12). This scripture speaks to the multiplication of impact when we support one another. If we want to be unstoppable, we cannot do it alone! We must find faithful friends to fight with us and for us.

WE NEED ONE ANOTHER

The truth is, no matter how strong you are, no matter how influential you are, no matter how important you may be, you need people.

Say that with me.

I need people.

Why is that so hard for some of us to say? Does it make you less of a person if you need help? Do you lose some imaginary points by admitting that you don't have all the answers?

For some reason, we have chosen to believe that we are better by ourselves—even when we know Jesus refused to live this way. He has always been a community within Himself: God the Father, God the Son, and God the Holy Spirit. This tells us something crucial about how God would have us live. The first "not good" in the Bible was in reference to Adam's situation. God looked upon Adam and said, "It is not good for the man to be alone. I will make a helper suitable for him" (Genesis 2:18, NIV).

God, from the beginning, knew that humanity was not made to be alone. It is in isolation that we see so many men and women fall. Yet for some reason, we all work our way toward being by ourselves.

I Don't Need Them, but I Would Love Them

This reminds me of a conversation I had with my dad. We were talking about the journey of growing up and getting older, and I made an observation. As children, we're dependent on our parents. We need their help with everything: making food, getting dressed, going to school. But somewhere along the way, we begin to deviate. We go from needing our parents for everything to trying to prove to them and everybody else that we do not need them—or anybody for that matter. It starts around our early teens and increases as we go through high school and into our twenties. But as we approach our mid-thirties, we realize we may not *need* our parents, but we do *want* them. We would like their advice, their help, their care and support. The cycle brings us back to the people we need most.

This has been true with both my family and friends. There have been moments when I felt the need to prove that I didn't need anybody; I was fine by myself. I believed I was strong enough, capable enough, and confident enough. If someone didn't like me, it didn't bother me. But nothing could have been further from the truth.

Though I was trying to prove I didn't need anybody, I wanted somebody.

I wanted someone to care, someone to talk to, someone to share ideas with, someone to be there when I celebrated my greatest moments. Even if we don't want to admit it, we all need someone.

We want someone to share memories with. We want someone to share love and laughter with. And if you'll look around, you'll notice that God has planted people in your life—friends, one of the most beautiful gifts ever given to man.

Friends are different from family. You can't choose your family. You're stuck with your crazy cousins, wild aunts, and that one person who always shows up to the cookout. But friends are different—friends, you choose. God not only chose you, but He also chose you for the people you're around.

GRANNY ESTELLE'S WISDOM

I started this chapter with my granny's amazing quote: "If you hang with nine broke friends, you are bound to be the tenth one."

This idea is true when it comes to any friendship. If you hang with nine people who have a bad attitude, you're bound to be the tenth. If you hang with nine friends who don't have integrity, you're bound to lower your standards. If you hang with people who have no vision for their lives, you will slowly lose direction. If you hang with people who give little thought to how they live, you will find yourself becoming someone you never thought you would be.

The beautiful thing about Granny's wisdom is that it also works the opposite way. If you hang with people who have standards, you will begin raising the bar for yourself. If you hang with people who pray, you'll find yourself praying and believing God can do amazing things. If you hang with people who are actively pursuing God rather than money, you will grow wiser and more concerned with what God thinks than with what others think.

Your friends have more power in your life than you realize. I would submit that right after your spouse, your friends are some of the most important people to foster or deter your calling.

God with Skin On

In 2017, I DMed a guy I met on Instagram. He was preaching with a hip-hop beat behind a sermon, and I recognized him from seeing his younger brother at some of our services. His name was Michael Todd. I asked him if we could go to coffee because I had some questions about ministry and church. I was only a few years in and had no idea what I was doing.

I'll never forget our meeting. He was wearing a purple suit jacket and green pants on a Tuesday morning. Who does that? My friend Michael Todd, that's who. I would soon learn that was nothing unusual. And I love that about him. There in that coffee shop, I was meeting a man who would become one of my very best friends. I expected Mike to ask me a bunch of questions about ministry, but instead he asked me about Abby.

He asked me what type of husband I was. He inquired about the integrity I was keeping and how I was maintaining a pure spirit. He spent an hour and a half checking on me. A month later we met again. I was equipped with my list of questions. And once again he ignored all my questions and started checking on me, my marriage, and my health. I learned that this was his pattern. He would always ignore what seemed like the most important thing, just to check on me.

Mike was showing me what it meant not to be a leader but a

friend. From the moment I met him, he showed himself to be a friend first, a pastor second, and a brother third. I love this about Mike. He's loud and a little crazy. He believes in God and has crazy faith. He shows up when it matters, and he shows up big and bold. He's there when I need him, when I don't know who else to talk to. He's a good friend. But he's not the only good friend I've made in the last couple of years.

Brie is like the Holy Spirit personified. Her presence brings peace and joy. She is kind, silly, and wise. She's shown me so much about God's grace and encouragement.

Then there is Aaron—the big brother I never knew I needed. He's a rock, he's safe, and he's hilarious. He gives me permission to be honest and is not intimidated by my brokenness. A true friend.

Carl and Laura have become some of our closest friends. They are safe, and they help my wife and me navigate the journeys of life.

My little brother, Chandler, and his wife, Lori, are our friends.

What am I trying to say?

Stop and take inventory. What friends do you have in your life? Who has God intentionally placed around you to add to you?

The Bible says, "Faithful are the wounds of a friend; profuse are the kisses of an enemy" (Proverbs 27:6, ESV).

Close friends are honest with you. They'll tell you the truth; they'll tell you when you're living beneath your purpose. We all need good friends. We need people in our corner. Perhaps you're in a season where you don't see anybody, where you don't have the relationships you feel you need, where it seems like everyone has abandoned you. I have good news. Jesus is your friend. And He is "a friend who sticks closer than a brother" (Proverbs 18:24, ESV).

It's a wild thought to imagine Jesus as your friend. He's holy, yes. He's sovereign, yes. He's the King, but He's also a friend. And friends want to talk. Friends want to laugh. Friends want to hear about your day. Friends want to know your fears. Friends want to know the dreams you're too scared to tell anybody else. A good friend will sit and listen and not try to fix you. I have never met a friend like Jesus.

There's an old hymn that I love that says,

There's not a Friend like the lowly Jesus:
No, not one! no, not one![2]

If you're lonely today, know that you have a friend, and He's near. My prayer for you is that Jesus would open your eyes to earthly friends, that you would look around and see people who maybe aren't perfect but would make great friends.

The greatest friends I've had are not those I simply shared interests with or who looked like me, voted like me, or talked like me. The greatest friends I've had were people who God placed in my life for a reason. If you find yourself wondering why God put these people around you, could it be that God sent the right people into your life to save you? I already mentioned it before, but in different seasons, I've had friends who have saved my life.

On-Time Friends

Every time I went to a new school and didn't know how I was going to fit in, I made a friend who kept me showing up and saved my life.

When I was a youth pastor and felt insecure in my calling, I had a friend who encouraged me and reminded me that I was called to this.

When I was getting married and didn't know how to be a husband of integrity and was fighting pornography, I had a friend who was vulnerable enough to tell me about his struggle, which gave me the strength to keep fighting.

When I was questioning ministry and whether I wanted to stick it out, I had a friend who called out the greatness in me and would not let me throw in the towel.

When I was having panic attacks and couldn't sleep, I had friends who showed up in the middle of the night to pray with me and support me.

When I have a wild thought and don't know where to place it, I have a friend I can text it to for guidance.

To Find a Friend, Be a Friend

Some of you may be discouraged as you read this chapter. Maybe you've thought, *I don't have friends like that.* If you have never had the joys of experiencing a real friend, I am so sorry. However, I encourage you to be the friend you so desperately need.

Proverbs 18:24 says, "A man who has friends must himself be friendly" (NKJV). If you have struggled to find the right people, perhaps focus on becoming the right person. If you're looking for friends of integrity, be a friend of integrity. If you're looking for friends who check on you, be the friend who checks on people. If you're looking for friends who don't gossip, be the friend who shuts down conversations that aren't uplifting. You can choose today to look for friends and be the friend who others need.

God chose you, but God also chose them. And that means God chose us. And trust me, we are better together.

Chapter 15

It's Never Too Late to Come Home

Come to me, all you who are weary and burdened, and I will give you rest. Take my yoke upon you and learn from me, for I am gentle and humble in heart, and you will find rest for your souls. For my yoke is easy and my burden is light.
—Jesus, Matthew 11:28–30, NIV

This is not the last chapter of my book, but this is the last chapter I wrote.

Honestly, the writing process has been far more daunting than I ever expected. I started off extremely confident, but as my deadlines grew closer and closer, I realized I would have to fight for a book I believed was worth putting out into the world. As it stands, I have come to discover a joy, genius, and beauty of writing that have honestly captivated my soul.

I read, reread, wrote, and rewrote so many chapters, so many sentences, so many paragraphs. But this chapter is different. This chapter is close to my heart.

I saved this one for last because, for some reason, it feels the most important. This chapter holds a lot of weight in my heart. Holds a lot of weight in my soul. Within this chapter, I want to have a conversation with you.

Just for a moment, forget that this is a book; forget all the tips you've read in previous chapters. Forget that I'm an author and pastor. For a moment, let's talk as friends. I want to talk to you in the way I wish I could talk to so many people I love.

This chapter was written for someone very specific. It's for those of you who don't know how or why you are reading a book with "God" in the title. This chapter is for those of you for whom the very name of God produces anger, disappointment, frustration, pain, or emptiness. It's for those of you who do not call yourself a Christian, or maybe you do but you aren't sure how much longer you will.

Perhaps you find yourself wandering on this planet aimlessly, too tired to bother with the question of whether there is a higher power. This chapter was written for you.

This chapter hinges on one question: If God Chose Me, then why has all this happened in my life?

As I was titling the chapters of my book, this question stuck out more than any other.

This is not a book for just Christians. As a matter of fact, my personality is usually bent toward trying to offend Christians just a little bit (in love) because that's what I feel Jesus would have done. I pray this book somehow makes its way to the outsiders, to the "nobodies," to the misfits, to the people who feel like they're too far gone, too broken, too hurt, too dirty to be touched by God. If that describes you, I want to talk to you for just a moment.

I'm not sure what you've heard about God or what experiences you have had in church or with Christians. Statistics would tell me that you've probably had some horrible encounters. You've been manipulated, used, and hurt by people who claim the Jesus that I claim. I want to take a moment to say I'm sorry. I'm sorry that happened. I'm sorry others abused their power. I'm sorry it left you confused, hurt, and broken.

I am sorry, and you can still come home.

I know what you must be thinking: *How can you know where my home is? You don't know me.* You're right—I don't know you. But I do know who created you, and the truth is, your home is with Him. You are not made to be alone in your pain. You are not made to be alone in your shame. Your home is with God.

Your First Home

In the book of Genesis, we are given a glimpse into God's perfect plan. It's a beautiful garden full of the most beautiful vegetation ever seen. It's perfect. There is everything that we need: peace, love, joy, acceptance, purpose, and most importantly, God's presence. It was meant to be the one place where heaven and earth collide. It was the place where humanity and divinity intersected. It was the place with the sole purpose of relationship building, intimacy forming, and love sharing between a creator and creation. It was our original home. It was a picture of God's intention for human beings. It was His perfect design, His creation with purpose, as we subdued, ruled, and guided with Him walking by our side, hand in hand with us, through all of life.

However, because of the Enemy's plan and our own decisions, sin entered the world. The word *sin* is originally an ancient term. It means "to miss the mark." It's expanded to mean "rebellion," "mistakes," "pain," "hurt"—all the things wrong about the world. Sin entered the world and it caused the greatest divide. It ruined the beauty, love, and intimacy we shared with God. It tore us out of our home and flung us into a desert, a place filled with thorns and pain, tears and brokenness, murder, molestation, and starvation. Ever since that day, it has been man's plight to be ripped out of our home and subjected to things we were never supposed to experience.

From that moment, we have all been in no-man's-land, wandering this earth, searching for things we had at our disposal in the garden: affirmation, love, contentment, truth, happiness, fulfillment, health, wholeness, peace, dreams, hope, and light. Everything we so desperately search for today, God gave us freely in our home—but now we are far from that home.

We have wandered so far for so long, some of us can't even recognize the path that would lead us home, and maybe that's where you find yourself today. You're not at home and you know it. Perhaps you've tried to act like you love this life and you are perfectly content. You've convinced yourself that you don't have questions or fears or worries. Deep down, however, you know something's missing. You know there must be something more. You know you weren't meant to live this way. But you've been away from home for so long you don't even know what's back there. Even if you wanted to go back, you wouldn't know which way to turn. So it's easier to stay away from home—to even vilify home—than it is to admit that deep down you really want to go back. I'm not sure how you got where you are. What I do know is you can still come home.

How do I know?

Jesus told a story in the Scriptures about a young man who found his way home.

A Tale of Two Sons

In Luke 15, Jesus told a story about two sons. One day, the younger son came to his father and essentially told him, "Dad, I'm done doing it your way. I want my inheritance now, and I want to live my own life." Though surely shocked at his younger son's demand, the father obliged. He gave his son his inheritance, and the son went on his way. He eventually ended up in the equivalent of Las Vegas or Miami and had the greatest time ever—money, sex, drugs, the biggest parties. He lived it up. He did what he wanted, when he wanted, with whom he wanted.

That is, until he ran out of money. And when you run out of money, you begin to run out of friends. He went from being the life of the party to the kid who couldn't find help, friends, or a job. Jesus tells us that the son got so low that he asked a farmer for work and even began imagining eating the scraps that he fed to the pigs. He went from the mountaintop to the valley quicker than he could blink. The world had served him up a harsh dose of reality, and he was struggling. As he contemplated whether to eat the pigs' food, it hit him: Maybe he could go home, not as a son but as a servant.

He knew there was no way he could go home as a son. For him to have asked his father for his inheritance was essentially to say, "Dad, I wish you would die already. Give me my money." He had made too many bad decisions to be accepted back as a son, but maybe his dad would have enough grace in his heart to accept him as a servant. He could work hard, keep his distance, and maybe, just maybe, get some food that was better than pig slop.

He prepared an apology, a long list of the ways he'd wronged his father, and slowly began to drag his feet back toward home. We don't know how long the journey was, but I can only imagine the questions, fears, doubts, and hesitation as he second-guessed what his father's response would be. *He's going to be angry. He's going to be so hurt and probably immediately reject me. He'll be so frustrated—will he even look at me? He'll probably just send me back out. I've got to live with the consequences. It's the only reasonable response.*

As the boy made his way home, he finally approached his father's land and saw the house in the distance. Sitting on the front porch was his father. And that's where the focus of our story shifts.

Every single day the boy's father had sat waiting for this day—the day his son came home. The story tells us that while the boy was still far away, the father peered into the distance and saw a small shadow. He knew it was his son. He'd observed that boy's shoulders since he was a toddler. He knew how the boy hung his head when he'd been hurt. It was him. He knew it. So, what did the father do? He didn't fold his arms and scowl. No, he took off in a dead sprint, completely contrary to the social norm. He ran for his son.

As the boy saw his father running, I can only imagine how he began to brace himself for a harsh conversation. But he was met with the exact opposite. His dad threw himself onto his son, wrapping his arms around him, crying, "I've missed you! I love you! I was so worried about you. Are you okay? Do you need anything? Come here. Let's get you inside. Let's get you some food. Take my ring, take my robe."

The son was stunned. He couldn't believe it. Why was his dad doing this? He was a bad person. He was a bad son.

"No, Dad, you don't understand. I'm sorry. I just . . . I just want to be a servant."

"Be quiet, son."

"But, Dad—"

"I said, be quiet."

His dad brought him inside, restored him as a son, prepared a feast, and celebrated his boy who was lost and had come home.

Have You Left Home?

If you feel far from home, it's okay. I'm not sure what your journey was like. I'm not sure why you left.

Maybe you left because you wanted to see what the world had to offer. Maybe you left because someone who said they loved you hurt you. Maybe you left because you had questions the pastor wasn't answering. Maybe you left because this faith thing is just too hard. Maybe you didn't want to leave but you felt like you had no other option. I'm not sure what took you away from home, but I am confident that it's not too late to return.

You see, when you get far away from home, it's easy to think that you're so far away you could never come back—that there's no way you could be restored, no way the Father would love you, no way He would ever overlook all the things that you have done. My friend, that is a lie. In fact, any voice that tells you that you cannot come home is directly from hell. I don't usually give hell a lot of credit, but in this case, it gets all of it. The Bible tells us that the single goal of the devil is to steal, kill, and destroy (see John 10:10). From the very beginning, he has hated you, and he specifically hates the fact that you would ever find out that God loves you. So, what does the devil do? He spends his life selling lies and deceit, fear, worry, and insecurity. He does whatever he can to rip you out of the one place you were designed to fit: home. It's been his plan since he lied to Eve. It was his plan in the Old Testament. It was his plan in the New Testament. It has been his plan this year. Right now, as you read, he wants to do whatever he can, however he can, to keep you from the truth that God loves you, cares about you, and accepts you just as you are.

If I could, I would sit down right now with you personally. I would ask you questions like, "Why don't you believe, and why did you walk away?" And then I would do one of the most powerful things any human being can do: listen.

I understand you have valid reasons why you don't believe, valid reasons why you don't trust pastors like me, valid reasons why it's hard to believe the Bible or hard to believe that there's a God who actually is involved and invested in your life.

Just look at history. Christians—the very group of people I have addressed this book to—have used the Bible to enslave, manipulate, hurt, and so much more. I'm not ignoring the fact of what's happened. The truth is, Christianity has a rocky past when it comes to humans trying to represent the divine, but I want to be very clear with you—do not impose the mistakes of man onto the character of God.

It is true that man is messed up. It is true that there has been manipulation and mistakes made and misrepresentations of God.

Regardless of what man does, God is still good. God is kind, God is gracious, God is loving, God is accepting. God is holy. God cares about you and the pain you're experiencing. And no matter what people have told you, no matter who has abandoned you, and no matter how they have misrepresented His love, do not allow the mistakes of people to rob you of living in your true home. The one place you truly belong.

Do not allow a moment of fear or hurt to rob you of being in the very place you were created to be, and that is with God.

You may read these words and still want nothing to do with God. Let me just ask: Do you enjoy the life you have? Do you like how you feel? Have you found peace? Do you have joy? Do you know who you are? Do your friends like you for you? Do you feel purpose? How do you handle pain? What do you do with anxiety? What hope do you have for tomorrow?

Do You Love Your Life?

You can keep the life you have, with the same fears, worries, and anxieties—or you can try something new.

Maybe the reason you avoid God is because you have lied to yourself about the quality of life you're living. You've painted a rosy picture of yourself as if you have no questions, you love your situation, and you have everything you need. But the truth is for some, when you slow down long enough to feel the pain inside of you, you realize your soul is fractured to a point that money, sex, drugs, and influence cannot fix.

So, what do you do? You are at a crossroads. You have a choice to make: You can either admit that you are completely broken and your life is empty, or you can continue to pile on the things that you know will not fix it. This is not easy. It takes humility to admit you went the wrong way. It takes humility to admit that you are broken. It takes humility to admit you want to come home. Friend, please do not allow yourself to stay stuck in what you know you do not want just because you do not want to admit how much you miss home.

I know you've experienced hurt. I know you've been through hardship. I know you're worried about what it's going to cost you—but come home.

You'll be surprised at what happens when you arrive. You won't be met with shame or guilt. You'll be met with a hug, grace, and mercy. You'll be met by the God who knows the deepest, darkest secrets of your life. He knows what has happened to you. He knows what you've been through. He knows how deeply you hurt and how much you've missed Him, and all He wants is to restore you to your true identity.

It makes sense, once you've made a bunch of mistakes, to settle for a servant. And the truth is, there are a lot of people who follow Jesus who have settled for servant. By that, I mean settling to be a hired hand instead of a loved child. Their whole walk with Him is built on this false humility and shame that keeps them stuck with their head down and no hope. They go to church and read the Bible out of duty. They pray because it's what you're supposed to do and live in a perpetual state of purgatory, trying to punish themselves for the mistakes they've made.

The only problem is, when you live like this, you cheapen grace. You rob God of the very gift He died to give you on the cross. The Bible tells us that Jesus did all the work for us, and when we live otherwise, we cheapen the cross and tell God, "Your sacrifice wasn't enough. I know You died and were beaten until You were unrecognizable, but that wasn't enough for me. It wasn't enough for what I've done. The mistakes I've made. The people I've hurt."

Imagine that your car is completely worn out and broken down. It will barely start each morning, and you can't drive farther than three miles without it overheating. This was the case for my first car. Imagine a generous stranger sees your plight, goes to the dealership, and buys you a brand-new car. It's your dream car, completely paid off, insurance covered, taxes paid, and maintenance already scheduled. They walk up to you and hand you the keys. But instead of accepting and living in this new reality, you reject it. You even throw the keys back in their face, saying, "I don't want this new car. I don't deserve it. I'll just have to struggle, be late, and stay where I am."

Sometimes it's hard to receive grace. Sometimes we feel unworthy or like we need to earn it. *That is not the gospel.* That may be how it worked with your parents, your friends, your co-worker, your boss, maybe even at your church, but that is not the heart of God. Grace is freely given and not earned. There's nothing you could do—even if you worked your whole life. But the Bible tells us that God sent Jesus to be the atonement and to completely cover the cost of our mistakes. God simply asks us to receive this extravagant gift.

God does not want you to settle for a servant. He wants to restore you as a son, as a daughter. You see, a son or daughter has an inheritance, a son or daughter has authority, a son or daughter has identity.

If I could drag you home, I would. But I heard someone once say, the way you catch them is the way you've got to keep them, so I know dragging you won't work.

And I'm not going to promise that if you to come to Jesus He'll fix your problems. I'm not going to convince you to come to Jesus to try to trick you, like everything's going to be perfect. But I will tell you that He's the only person who knows what you're feeling. He's the only person who can help you. He's the only person who knows everything you've been through and still loves you. He's your only hope. You need Him. Will you come home?

If you want to live an unstoppable life, you must first know the Savior. I don't know your situation. Maybe you have money in the bank, or maybe you don't have a dollar to your name. Maybe you're living your dreams, or maybe life seems to have passed you by. Wherever you are, the Bible says, "Now is the day of salvation" (2 Corinthians 6:2). If you feel alone—as though you cannot take the pressures of this life—you need a Savior. If you are tired of running, surrender. In your heart, mind, and soul: surrender. The Bible tells us that the moment you surrender your life to Christ, you have a fresh start (2 Corinthians 5:17). If you need a relationship with Jesus, simply say "I need You." Don't wait. Tell Him now. He is waiting for you to call out to Him. He will save you and transform you. That doesn't mean everything will be perfect, but it does mean you will be home.

Friend, we've been waiting for you. Welcome back.

Chapter 16

UNTOUCHABLE

You did it! You made it to the final chapter. I'm proud of you.

You may have put this book down and picked it back up several times, or you may have just powered your way through—but either way, you were strong, consistent, and you finally made it to the very end. We've covered a lot of content. We've talked about the importance of identity, acceptance, and love. We've talked about how to stay ready, ridiculous, reverent, resilient, and remembering. We've also talked about the importance of relationships. I've exposed my heart in this book, and hopefully you have too. You've done a lot of work—inner work, outer work, mental work, relational work. You've made it to the end in the hope that there is a better tomorrow. I believe that if you will truly accept and live like God chose you, He will ignite something inside of you that will unlock a life you have only dreamed of. But I have a confession to make.

I Hope This Book Changes You

As much as I believe this book can change you, I can't *promise* this book will change you.

Do I believe this book can change people? Yes, I'm 100 percent confident of that. Why? Because it has changed me. The process of writing has made me wrestle with what I really believe. It's made me face real challenges. It's made me ask myself why God Chose Me. It made me question whether I believe what I am writing. So, yes, I do believe this book can change you—but I cannot promise it will. Why? Because it's just paper. It's ink, a little bit of hard work, and my thoughts. My amazing publishing team printed it and put it on the bookshelf or on the website. And now it's in your hands. You're reading it. But eventually you're gonna put this book down. The words will slowly fade. You won't remember all my stories, and it'll be just you and your thoughts. The truth is, you'll probably still have the same struggles you had before you picked up this book. Some of the same insecurities will still be there. You'll still find yourself struggling with the same cycles.

This book can change your life, but you're the only one who can decide if it will.

We've all read books. We've all heard beautiful things. If I were to ask you what you need to do to get six-pack abs, you could probably put together some form of a functional plan. Eat right, do crunches, get good sleep, drink water. And if you did those things consistently, over time, you'd have a solid core. However, as we sit with this book, how many of us have rock-hard abs? It's not for a lack of knowledge; it's for a lack of application.

We all know what we need to do to be on time. We all know what it takes to have a good marriage. If you ask anyone what it takes to live a healthy life, I'm confident enough in humanity that they could put together some sort of answer that would be truthful. You see, we do not suffer from a lack of knowledge. In fact, today we have access to more knowledge than ever before.

The human mind was not meant to have access to this much knowledge. There is no way our frail little minds were meant to know what was happening on every inch of the earth at every second of the day. No wonder our anxiety is through the roof. No wonder we live in a constant state of fear and worry. We have too much knowledge!

On the other hand, there's nothing that forces us to apply the knowledge. We can simply post what we just googled, and nobody's confirming if we actually did what we just said. We keep our distance and we keep moving. I mean, there are actually people who make money on social media by researching stuff, pretending they've known it for a long time, buying a domain and a mic, and recording a podcast telling you what they just found out. It's ludicrous.

In our day of instant information, there is a huge gap between what we say and what we do, what we believe and how we act. It is the perfect storm that widens the gap between the life we desire and the life we lead. This constant battle, this constant struggle, leaves us feeling empty and worthless—like we cannot trust ourselves.

I once read *The Speed of Trust* by Stephen Covey, which asserts that trust with others starts with self-trust.[1] Covey claimed it would be more beneficial for you to set an alarm for 8:00 A.M. rather than 7:15 and then hit Snooze for forty-five minutes. The idea is that you must build the muscle of trust with yourself before you can build it with others. I believe this provides crucial insight into how we should live. For any true information we encounter, it is not enough to just read and understand; we must do something about it.

We don't need more knowledge. We need more revelation. We need revelation that turns into action. We need action that turns into a lifestyle. We need a lifestyle that is upheld by systems, and we need systems that are rooted in a source greater than ourselves. We need something more than just self-help and a couple of good ideas to get us through the week. We need something that changes the way we live, the way we talk, the way we breathe. My friend, this book can change you. But the question is, Will you allow it to change you?

WILL YOU LET IT CHANGE YOU?

Will you allow the message in this book to go beyond just something cute that you read one time or something that you bought or heard? Will you allow it to become something that you put into practice daily? Will you allow it to be something that shapes the way you talk, not only to yourself but to those around you? Will you allow this book to go beyond just words and become something that you build your life on? Will you allow these words to become something that means enough to you to change you right now?

I am just a man, and these are just words. As much as I believe in this message, I am also self-aware enough to know that there is nothing magical about what I've written. Maybe I've said some things that feel fresh, but the idea of you being chosen by God is not mine. It originates before time began.

At best, what I hope you receive from this book is a fresh perspective and a new outlook on life. A new way to relate to your situation, your problems, and your hardships. A new anchor for your soul so that—as we have addressed with the six anchors and seven attitudes—you can now begin to enter the space every human soul deeply desires: the unique grace at the intersection of confidence and contentment.

THE DYNAMIC DUO: CONFIDENCE AND CONTENTMENT

Confidence: A sense of sureness, readiness, humility, and inner strength. Not born from self but received from God. The ability to step out and look crazy. It is trust in God that is so deeply ingrained in you that you are prepared to do whatever He asks, whenever He asks, wherever He asks. To walk with your head held high, never down. To look toward tomorrow with faith and not fear. To believe the best of people and God. To be willing to take the risk to believe Him and have the boldness to trust Him. This is the confidence I speak of.

Contentment: A settled soul. A rested mind. A heart that needs nothing more than to simply be with God. No need to strive or work harder or do more. No sense of lack or fear of missing out. Just a deep sense of gratitude and appreciation for the moment you're in and where you are.

What would it be like to live here? What would your life look like if each day you woke up extremely confident and content. If you woke up with boldness, asking, "God, what are we doing today, and how are we gonna change the world?" If you had the contentment to say, "God, I'm good if I just go to work today, come home, have a good meal, and get to wake up tomorrow."

This life-changing combination of confidence and contentment is the deepest desire of my soul. It is where I want to live. It's how I want my kids to see their dad live his life. It's what I want them to see when they look at their mother. It's what I want deep inside of them.

Metcalfs are confident and Metcalfs are content.

We don't need anything else from anyone. We live boldly, we take risks, we trust God, and we are fine if God never gives us another thing.

The Only Answer to Every Question

For a while this was going to be the subtitle for my book: "The Only Answer to Every Question." In my early stages of writing, a friend came up with this line. When he originally said it, we were both impressed—and then never thought about it after that. But it is a statement that operates as ultimately true. Because of the work of Jesus, because He has defeated death, we can trust that no matter what we are facing, we can find the answer to our questions in Him! *He* is the answer to every question.

Why is this happening? *God Chose Me.*

Am I gonna make it? *Yes, God Chose Me.*

How am I gonna make it? *God Chose Me.*

Can I do this? *God Chose Me.*

Nothing could be truer. Any question you face, this truth can answer.

The Untouchable

As I sit here making the final edits to my first book, I am full of joy and gratitude. This book has pastored me, coached me, corrected me, and inspired me as I have written it. As I said earlier, when I started this book I had no idea where I was going. But now, as I type this final section, I realize that it is the grace and kindness of God that has brought me to this place. It is because of the gospel—the finished work of Jesus—that I can write this book with peace in my soul. I have spent many nights wondering and worrying about the success of this book. Will it sell? Will people like it? At one time those thoughts held me captive. They drove me to write from a place of not wanting to "screw up my big break." However, along the way something new was birthed in me. It is a confidence that is not connected to the success of this book. A confidence that is untouchable. Money can't touch it. People's opinions can't touch it. My own fears can't touch it. Why? Because it comes from the fact that God Chose Me to write this book. And that is enough.

As we end our journey, I pray this message is wind in your sails. I pray this belief is fire in your bones. I pray that your sense of self finds its anchor deep below the shallow counterfeits this world has to offer. I pray comparison feels as useless as a sweater in August. That your mind is as free as a bird in springtime. I pray your heart beats strongly as one that is full of purpose. That your eyes see beyond tomorrow and into the legacy you leave behind. That your voice carries a strength that is not shaken by the world's systems and structures. That you would get in your bag day in and day out. That you would share the radical message of Jesus and let it transform your community. That you would stand firm for the Word of God. That you would dream big dreams and leave no gift unturned. That, like the early church, you would believe that the message of Jesus is so real it's worth dying for. That you would stare fear in the face and never back down. That you would find your strength and source in Christ alone. That you would raise your family to know the stories of Yahweh. That you are blessed to see the Water-walker for yourself. That you would live each day fully, with your head held high and your shoulders back. That you would know deep in your soul this foundational truth and reality with which all things move:

God Chose Me.

I love you,

Charles.

A Letter to Little Charles

Dear Charles,

Hey, it's me. Well, it's you, but it's me.

I'm writing you this letter to let you know everything's going to be okay.

It is the year 2024 and you're finishing writing your first book.

It's full of hope, confidence, power, conviction, and assurance—all things that feel impossible from your perspective.

The origins of this book are many; however, I must first address the free throw. Yes, the free throw. For most of your life you have looked at that moment as the moment that reinforced all of your greatest fears. However, with some time and perspective, you will learn that everything you focused on in that moment is actually a strength, not a weakness.

You will experience many ups and downs in life as you move forward; however, the emotion and fear of that moment will stay with you and lead you to some challenging places. The one that plants the seeds of this message happens on April 27, 2020.

You will find yourself curled up under your desk, writing in a journal. You're confused, you're afraid. You can't turn off your negative thoughts. You're fearful of what you might do. I want to let you know everything's going to be okay. You're going to talk to your friends and to your wife, Abby. You're not going to take your own life, and you're not going to cheat on your spouse. You're not going to go down the path that feels inevitable at that moment.

In fact, it will be a turning point for you—the pressure and the depression you feel in that moment will form deep within you. It will cut away fears and insecurities to produce a diamond, something worth infinite value—not to be displayed to the world, but to be treasured by you. On the inside, you're going to start working through some things. You're going to see a counselor. You're going to have to be honest about your weakness. You're going to have to talk to Abby and tell her what's really going on in your head and your heart. You're going to have to be honest with your friends. You will have more panic attacks. They get worse before they get better. You're even going to have one while you're preaching. It's going to terrify you. You'll be worried that it's going to happen more and more, and that thought will make you more and more panicky.

But you'll gradually make it through the panic attacks. They'll slowly drift away, and you'll start to see health a few short months later.

I can't tell you all the details, but you'll have a near-death experience. You'll be carted away in an ambulance having a seizure, and, looking your wife and friend in the eyes, you will think, this is it. It's not; you just need to drink more water, dummy.

You will have a son, Arlo. He is smart, inquisitive. He has more questions than you have answers, but it's good that way. You're going to have three more beautiful babies, all girls, and they will bring so much sass and joy into your life. You and Abby are going to become closer than you ever have been before. The pressure and the pain will actually draw you together.

Mimi's going to pass away. It's going to be hard on Abby. It'll test your marriage and your faith, but God will see you through.

I'm writing you this letter to tell you I'm proud of you—proud of the work you've done, proud of the man that you are. You've had mo-ments to sacrifice your integrity, to fall to your lesser self, but you don't do it. You're not perfect. You make mistakes, but you're a good man. God's hand is on your life. You're going to make it through. You and one of your friends are going to write a sermon called "God Chose Me." You'll have no idea as you're preaching it, but it's the seed of something that's going to ripple around the world. It's going to erupt in that room, and you will watch it spread and bear fruit.

It'll be the very fire shut up in your bones. It's gonna change ev-erything. You're going to get a book deal and become an author, Charles. You're really gonna do it. It's gonna change your family line. You don't have to be afraid, you don't have to worry, you don't have to do anything other than what you've always done. Say yes to God.

You can do this, Charles. God's with you.

He's called you. He chose you.

A lot is gonna change, and nothing's gonna change. All you need to do right now is take it one day at a time, trust God, and be faith-ful. The plan He has is so beautiful—there's so much peace, fun, and joy in following His way. He didn't make a mistake and He didn't miss it—in fact, you are right on track.

Strangely enough, you get hit by a car as your book deadlines ap-proach. It takes your writing timeline from eight weeks to three. Sounds insane, right? It is, but you're fine, you're healthy. And of course, you get back on your bike.

You stay up all night to finish the book, but it's good. It's really good. Like really good. I don't know this for sure, but something tells me you will write many books that change the world.

Proud of you, kid. You did a good job.

You're gonna make it.

Love you, bud. See you in a few years.

Acknowledgments

To my wife, the love of my life and my safe place. You believed in me when I couldn't. You are my dream. ILYB.

To Arlo, Luna, Jade, and Blue. I love you so very much. You have made your mom and dad's lives a dream. I am so proud of who you are. I am here for you always.

To my mom and dad. Thank you for being the first people to ever see and believe that God Chose Me. You instilled a God-given confidence in me that became the seed of this book.

To Chandler. You inspire me more than you know. Being your brother has made me a better follower of Jesus, friend, father, and man. WBBF, I love you, boy.

To Mike. You're better than a friend, you're better than a boss, you're better than a pastor. You're you. Thank you for sharing your life with me.

To all my extended family. Thank you for your love and support in my life. From Kentucky to Oklahoma, each one of you is a part of this story.

To Mimi and Poppi. I love you so much! Your grandson wrote a book.

To all my friends. You've saved my life in more ways than one, and I could never repay you.

To Transformation. Thank you for transforming me.

To the devil. Thanks for trying me. It made me.

To God. Thank You. I love You.

Notes

Chapter 2: THIS IS WHAT GOD DOES

1. Fr. Cajetan Mary da Bergamo, *Humility of Heart* (Veritatis Splendor, 2012), 6.

2. John Piper, "What Is the Sovereignty of God?," Desiring God, April 8, 2019, www.desiringgod.org/interviews/what -is-the-sovereignty-of-god.

Chapter 4: HE KNOWS YOU . . . AND HE STILL CHOSE YOU

1. By the way, that person was Erwin McManus. Sir, thank you. The conversation we had that day is a significant reason I began to write this book. Thank you for holding space for this kid. I couldn't articulate it when we met, but I now know the hug, laugh, tone, and frequency of a maven is rare. And when two of them meet, it's a beautiful thing. Thank you for making room and inspiring me to step creative to genius. I changed your name in my phone to "Leader of the Mavens."

2. Gary Portnoy and Judy Hart-Angelo, "Theme from *Cheers* (Where Everybody Knows Your Name)," Applause, 1983.

3. Vincent Mims, "That's My King by Dr. S. M. Lockridge," Stonebridge Church, April 16, 2012, gostonebridge.com /2012416thats-my-king-by-dr-sm-lockridge-html.

Chapter 5: THE REJECT EFFECT

1. Michael Todd, "The Disease of Double-Minded // Death to Distraction" (sermon, Tulsa, OK, delivered February 2, 2025), www.youtube.com/watch?v=rH2e5-zjDLY.

2. Mark R. Leary, "Emotional Responses to Interpersonal Rejection," *Dialogues in Clinical Neuroscience* 17, no. 4 (2015): 435–41, pubmed.ncbi.nlm.nih.gov/26869844.

Chapter 6: A SINGULAR SYMPHONY

1. "Largest Orchestra," Guinness World Records, accessed January 15, 2024, www.guinnessworldrecords.com/world -records/largest-orchestra.

Chapter 7: YOU'D BE SURPRISED WHAT A LITTLE BELIEF CAN DO

1. "I Believe I Can Fly" by R. Kelly, track 5 on *Space Jam* (Soundtrack), Universal Music, 1996.

Chapter 8: BETTER WATCH YOUR WORDS

1. Lindsey Horton, "The Neuroscience Behind Our Words," Business Relationship Management Institute, August 8, 2019, https://brm.institute/neuroscience-behind-words.

2. Horton, "Neuroscience Behind Our Words."

Chapter 9: READY WHEN YOU ARE

1. Bible Study Tools, s.v. "šāmayim," accessed January 4, 2025, www.biblestudytools.com/lexicons/hebrew/kjv /shamayim.html.

2. Karen Sottosanti, "Observable Universe," Britannica, November 23, 2024, www.britannica.com/topic/observable -universe.

3. Sottosanti, "Observable Universe."

Chapter 10: I'M NOT AFRAID TO LIVE

1. Michael Todd, *Crazy Faith: It's Only Crazy Until It Happens* (WaterBrook, 2021).

Chapter 12: GET UP, DONNIE!

1. *Oxford English Dictionary,* s.v. "resilience, n.," accessed January 15, 2024, www.oed.com/dictionary/resilience_n.

2. WebMD Editorial Contributors, "What Is Hematidrosis?," WebMD, April 7, 2024, www.webmd.com/a-to-z-guides /hematidrosis-hematohidrosis.

Chapter 13: ALL I NEED IS A MEMORY

1. Catherine Caruso, "A New Field of Neuroscience Aims to Map Connections in the Brain," Harvard Medical School, January 19, 2023, hms.harvard.edu/news/new-field -neuroscience-aims-map-connections-brain.

2. Valerie Ross, "Numbers: The Nervous System, From 268-MPH Signals to Trillions of Synapses," *Discover Magazine,*

May 14, 2011, www.discovermagazine.com/health
/numbers-the-nervous-system-from-268-mph-signals-to
-trillions-of-synapses.

3. Caruso, "A New Field of Neuroscience."

4. Kirk Franklin & the Family, "When I Think About Jesus,"
track 6 on *Whatcha Lookin' 4*, GospoCentric, 1995.

Chapter 14: MY FRIENDS SAVED MY LIFE

1. Sara Mandell, "Who Paid the Temple Tax When the Jews
Were Under Roman Rule?" Cambridge University Press,
June 10, 2011, www.cambridge.org/core/journals/harvard
-theological-review/article/abs/who-paid-the-temple-tax
-when-the-jews-were-under-roman-rule/E1E297F911D12
4CAE83C120B84CA3C4B.

2. Johnson Oatman, Jr., "No, Not One," 1895.

Chapter 16: UNTOUCHABLE

1. Stephen Covey and Rebecca Merrill, *The Speed of Trust: The
One Thing That Changes Everything* (Free Press, 2018).

About the Type

This book was set in Albertina, a typeface created by Dutch calligrapher and designer Chris Brand (1921–98). Brand's original drawings, based on calligraphic principles, were modified considerably to conform to the technological limitations of typesetting in the early 1960s. The development of digital technology later allowed Frank E. Blokland (b. 1959) of the Dutch Type Library to restore the typeface to its creator's original intentions.

From author and pastor
CHARLES METCALF

CHARLES H METCALF III

GOD CHOSE ME

UNTOUCHABLE CONFIDENCE FOR THE UNSTOPPABLE CHRISTIAN

Foreword by *New York Times* bestselling author Michael Todd

Learn to harness the power of your words, build meaningful relationships, and recover from life's setbacks. This transformative book offers a road map to living authentically and confidently, empowering you to fulfill your unique, holy purpose.

This companion study and discussion guide to *God Chose Me* will propel you toward your God-given purpose with joy and clarity. Discover how embracing your chosen status can revolutionize your self-perception and daily life.

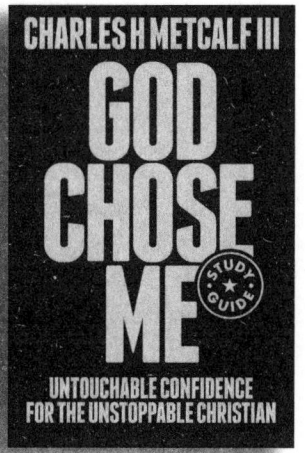

CHARLES H METCALF III

GOD CHOSE ME

STUDY GUIDE

UNTOUCHABLE CONFIDENCE FOR THE UNSTOPPABLE CHRISTIAN

WATERBROOK

Learn more about Charles Metcalf's books at
waterbrookmultnomah.com.

01 14